the
Clutter Cure

the
Clutter Cure

Three Steps to Letting Go of Stuff,

Organizing Your Space & Creating

the Home of Your Dreams

JUDI CULBERTSON

New York   Chicago   San Francisco   Lisbon   London   Madrid   Mexico City
Milan   New Delhi   San Juan   Seoul   Singapore   Sydney   Toronto

The *McGraw·Hill* Companies

Library of Congress Cataloging-in-Publication Data

Culbertson, Judi.
    The clutter cure : three steps to letting go of stuff, organizing your space, &
creating the home of your dreams / Judi Culbertson.
        p.   cm.
    Includes bibliographical references (p. 261–253) and index.
    ISBN 0-07-148744-1 (pbk.)
    1. Storage in the home.   2. Orderliness.

TX309 .C84   2007
640—dc22   2007279053

2 3 4 5 6 7 8 9 10 11 12 13 14 15 16 17 18 19 20 21 22 23 24   FGR/FGR   0 9 8

ISBN 978-0-07-148744-3
MHID   0-07-148744-1

Interior design by Nick Panos

McGraw-Hill books are available at special quantity discounts to use as premiums and sales
promotions or for use in corporate training programs. To contact a representative, please visit
the Contact Us pages at www.mhprofessional.com.

This book is printed on acid-free paper.

With love to the usual suspects—
Tom, Andy, Robin, Emily, and Andrew—
as well as to everyone brave enough
to undertake this journey.

Contents

Step 3: Take Action

Acknowledgments

It may take a world to publish a book, but special thanks go to my agent and friend, Linda Konner, and my wonderfully enthusiastic and competent editor, Johanna Bowman, as well as all the other people at McGraw-Hill whom I am just getting to know. Thanks also to my wonderful reader and friend, Adele Glimm, and my family and friends who had to keep hearing about the book. Finally, warm wishes to my past clients who opened their homes and souls to me and whose confidentiality I will continue to respect.

Introduction: Getting Started

"Why are you keeping *that* old thing?"

Cruel words! But you've probably heard them before. And guess what? Those people demanding to know have a point. Why *are* you holding on to those unread magazines, bread ties and plastic bags, baby gift cards, unused skis, or the beautiful wineglasses too fragile to use? How about that horrible aftershave, Jimmy Choo shoes that hurt your feet, and plans for a home you know you'll never build?

Too much stuff does more than clutter your life; it affects you emotionally, making it impossible to live with real freedom. But our relationship with our things is complicated. It involves a multitude of feelings, some of which we do not even realize. Yet until you understand the deep relationship you have with your belongings, and create an environment with only what you love and what represents your dreams, you'll stay stuck.

Now that I have your attention, here are some other things you need to know about stuff:

- Physical things can be seductive and attractive and hold the promise of a picture-perfect life.

- Stuff accumulates rapidly and gets dirty, breaks, takes up space, and hides what you need to find.
- Too much stuff confuses other people's idea of who you actually are, as well as your own self-image.
- Being overstuffed makes your life chaotic, unfocused, and frustrating.
- Just decluttering and organizing are not enough, and the traditional methods don't really work. If that is all you do, in a few months the desktop or garage floor will disappear again and you'll be discouraged and looking for another self-help book. Not only do you need to scale things down; you need to understand what you are doing and create a new and beautiful space that is easy to maintain.

Getting Emotional

Although I have worked as a professional organizer, I find the term misleading in my case. I don't help people fit things neatly into compartments or file cabinets. I try to help them get *rid* of their file cabinets or reduce them to just one. "Attacking clutter" without thought does not work for very long. I have learned that unless people recognize the emotional relationship they have with the physical world, they will be calling me year after year to bail them out.

My own wake-up call came in 1976 when my extended family rented a vacation house in Rehobeth Beach, Delaware. I was floored by the simplicity of the home. The kitchen held only the items we needed to prepare a meal. In the morning, after making the beds and washing the cereal bowls, we were done for the rest of the day. There was time to go to the beach, read, explore, or do anything else we wanted.

The Vacation House Feeling

I came home that August determined to have that "vacation house feeling" for the rest of my life. Except I couldn't imagine how. I had been a messy kid who grew into an adult with an accumulation of packed-away wedding gifts, hand-me-downs, books, art supplies, and beat-up furniture that I planned to turn into "antiques." I had a husband and child with their own paraphernalia. In addition, my mother was a frenetic shopper who gave presents constantly and expected to see them displayed.

I had no clue where to start. *Decluttering* was not yet a verb, and there were no TV shows about how to get organized. (Even when I started speaking on the subject in 1994, a lot of people had never heard the word *clutter* used to describe their accumulation.) After getting rid of the obvious junk and giving away excess, I started making lists. On the top of one column, I wrote "Item," and at the top of the next, "Why I'm Keeping It." Somehow, writing an item down clarified how I felt about it. If I wrote "Bridesmaid's dress" and in the second column "No reason good enough to save," I was able to give it away. When I came up against emotional resistance, I stopped and traced the reasons why I felt that way.

People in my workshops are always curious about whether I've achieved the vacation house feeling. Yes, I have. I live most of the time in a New York City two-bedroom apartment filled with art, books, and what I need for entertaining, a place that feels spacious. I know everything I own and where to find it quickly. Like the original beach house, my apartment requires very little care and leaves me time to do what I love.

When I first started giving lectures, people would come up to me afterward and beg me to declutter their homes. My background was in social work, and I still had a day job, but I took on the clients who seemed really desperate, using my own techniques. Eventually, I became a member of the National Association of Professional Organizers. Because I was helping a number of people prepare to move to condos and independent living situations where they would need much less stuff, another organizer, Marj Decker, and I wrote *Scaling Down: Living Large in a Smaller Space.*

Taking a New Approach

In *The Clutter Cure*, I use all of the same techniques that created exciting results for both me and my clients. I don't want you to start going at your things "cold," making off-the-cuff decisions and tossing items that you might miss later on. My goal is for you not only to get control over your stuff but also to understand what your "stuff" means to you and then move toward turning a lackluster or almost-there home into something wonderful—a place that you will love, use effectively, and take pride in.

The only equipment you'll need to start this process is a separate notebook (if you don't like writing in books or are working on the process with family members) and a collection of different colored dots from a stationery or office supply store. At the end of each chapter in the first section, you'll find prompts to help you identify the kinds of feelings the chapter has aroused. Throughout the book you will also find examples of "household endangered species." Whether it's a combination lock with the combination long forgotten or a "special occasion" item whose time will never come, these illustrations will give you insight into some of your own hangers-on.

Step 1: Identify

The first step in the three-step program is understanding our complicated emotional relationship to our physical world. On the one hand, things can be beautifully made, representative of our intelligence and personality, and part of our heritage. Having them around can make us happy and support our dreams. But what is sometimes hard to know is how to separate these treasures from all the other things that refuse to let us discard them when their natural life is over. There are many reasons why it is so hard, and I'll be discussing them in the first part of the book. You'll be looking at the things you own as they fit into one of eleven categories described in Chapters 1 through 11.

Step 2: Assess

After identification comes assessment. You'll be evaluating your rooms to decide what functions you want them to have and the mood and feeling you want to create. This is not about showing you photographs of beautiful spaces and encouraging you to re-create them. This is about starting with *your* home and writing mission statements to make it the best possible place for you. You will make lists of items you already have that contribute to the mood you want to create and those that don't and have to go. This is a good time to take some "before" photographs.

Step 3: Take Action

You make physical changes at this stage. Now that you have gained some psychological distance from the items you are ready to discard, you'll be able to quickly give away, sell, donate, or trash your household endangered species. All the information you need to do so is in this section.

As you work, it will be helpful to take "during" and "after" photographs and put them on the pages next to your "before" photographs.

At this point you may be tempted to think, "Why bother? I know I have too much stuff, so I'll just get rid of some of it." But you've tried that before—remember? Until you understand the underlying dynamics and *permanently* change your relationship to stuff, your decluttering will be short-lived. As soon as you hit an emotional roadblock, you'll decide that trying to get rid of stuff is hopeless. You'll give in to the voices that whisper

- "But you can always use that for _____."
- "You paid good money for this!"
- "How can you even think of getting rid of your _____?"
- "What would your mother say?"

And then you will feel discouraged and angry, because underneath you do know what you really want: a home that feels welcoming and serene, one that not only reflects who you are to the world but supports who you want to become. You want a home that doesn't leave you feeling panicked about having to straighten up when someone drops by, a place where you can settle in and feel happy and safe, a place that needs very little maintenance and leaves you time to spend doing what you really want. You may be tired of the conflict with other family members when things can't be found and they blame you.

There are other exciting benefits. As one feng shui tenet advises, "If you want to change your life, move twenty-two objects." Just the act of making small, successful changes can give you the confidence to take more crucial steps in your life. By creating physical and emotional space, you are making room for new experiences.

By the end of this book, you will either know why you are keeping "that old thing" or it will have found another home. You'll have an understanding of how "stuff" can be beautiful but emotionally confining and of how much more satisfying life is with less stuff. Most important, you will have created a space that is perfect for you and the ability to keep it that way.

End of lecture. Let's get started. If you want that vacation house feeling, it can be yours!

Step 1

—

Identify

1

"But It's Still Perfectly Good!"

I once knew a man who hoarded egg cartons. My father, actually. They were made of molded gray cardboard and perfect for holding old, nicked golf balls, which he also kept. My father saved mystery screws and loved the "box lots"—cartons of stuff too insignificant to be sold separately—he bought at auctions. Because he was good at fixing things, he also saved parts.

Yet as a graduate of the Coast Guard Academy in New London, Connecticut, he had learned to keep his possessions stowed neatly in a ship's small spaces. On land he kept them stowed neatly in a four-bedroom house, a double garage, a basement, an attic, a storage shed, and a rental space. It took us weeks to sort through the things he left behind after he died.

Sometimes when I was visiting I would ask, "Are you *really* going to use that?"

But he would just laugh. "You never know!"

Using it again wasn't even the point. The point was that it still had some good left in it. And anything with any good in it could *never* be thrown away.

People Are More Important than Stuff

Karyn, a vibrant but frustrated young woman, came to one of my early workshops; her situation reminded me of my father's. She felt that she had no choice but to sell the house her family had outgrown and buy a larger one in the countryside. The larger house even came with its own barn—a packrat's dream! But she wasn't happy about leaving the school district where her children were thriving, in a community that the whole family loved.

"You don't have to move," I told her. "It sounds as if it's a battle between people and stuff, and the stuff is winning."

"I know! But this is all good stuff. Could you come over and take a look? Maybe I'm just a packrat!"

We made an appointment, and I toured Karyn's house and sheds with her and her husband, Jay. I could see the way *I* had once been in the mountains of craft supplies she had accumulated, as well as the rescued furniture they were going to repair and sell and the hand-me-downs both sets of parents had bestowed on them. There were innumerable jars in the shed and every riding toy their children, now nine and eleven, had ever owned.

When we were done, to their surprise I asked them how they would use the rooms in their present house if they stayed, how they wanted them to feel. "You have much too much to assess every item as to whether it's still 'perfectly good' or not," I said. "You have to start from the top and pick out what actually contributes to your life now."

Karyn and Jay ended up staying in their three-bedroom home in the neighborhood to which they were so attached. Once she got into step three of the process, Karyn staged a series of yard sales and discarded everything that did not sell.

"You changed my life!" she told me whenever I saw her. But she and Jay were the ones who did that.

In the rest of the book, I'll explain in more detail what they—and other people—did. But back to the problem of "But it's still perfectly good!"

"Waste Not, Want Not"

People in my decluttering workshops often quote "Waste not, want not" to me. Actually, it's a motto that was popular as far back as 1722 and had an even earlier life as "Willful waste makes woeful want." Though it does not come from Shakespeare or the Bible, the precept has sticking power. For some people, *waste* means buying too much food and throwing the unused away. For people of my father's persuasion, tossing out a chipped ceramic cup becomes a moral issue. Who wants to be punished for discarding a used bread twist tie?

Here's how it goes. Even a chipped or handleless cup, if it doesn't leak outright, still has some good left in it. Perhaps it is unsightly and has been replaced by a cup whose rim won't scrape your lip, but it can always be used for something—to hold rescued shards of soap or the bacon fat you drain from the pan. Therefore, it should not be tossed wastefully away.

If "waste not, want not" resonates with you, you know what happens when you start to throw out an item too worthless to be given away (say, a half-used but stale can of poultry seasoning or the blocks of Styrofoam that came with a large purchase). You reach for them to say good-bye and then feel a creeping uneasiness, a shadow of guilt, as if you are about to do something wrong. Maybe you don't think about future retribution, but you don't feel *good* about tossing the item. When you put it back on the shelf or stick it in a drawer or closet, there's a sense of relief, of feeling virtuous, and of being thrifty.

But here's the problem. You've let vague feelings get the better of you. You know you will never *use* that seasoning again and that it will crowd the shelf, making it harder to find the spices you need. You have no immediate use for pieces of Styrofoam that size, and you probably know from experience how hard it is to cut it down without its crumbling into a million tiny white balls. These things will now conspire to make it impossible to locate the things you need—the things that other people are insisting that they have to have *right now*. When every inch of your life is packed, it is also impossible to think about making life changes and moving on to anything better.

Understanding Root Causes

What are the underlying reasons for the compulsion to hold on to anything that is "perfectly good"? In my father's case, there were several.

- He was one of six children whose mother, a schoolteacher, didn't work once she had a family. So thrift was a necessary family value.
- His mother was a packrat.
- He was on scholarship at a military academy when the Great Depression hit in 1929. He saw formerly employed men standing on street corners, trying to support their families by selling apples or pencils, and living in homeless camps. It was a terrible time that left him scarred.
- He came from a religious family in which the biblical precept of "good stewardship" meant not squandering anything.
- He was clever at fixing things and inventing new combinations, and when he used a part he had rescued, it gave him great satisfaction.

Why am I going on about my father? Because I encounter him—his attitudes, that is—over and over again in my workshops and with my clients. Many of the reasons for his underlying feelings—his memories of the Great Depression, a background in which saving was emphasized, thrift blended with religious belief, and the ability to find a new use for an old item—are exactly the same. If you identify with some of them yourself and, unlike my father, want to change your environment, the first step is to understand your underlying feelings.

You aren't unique, by the way. In my workshops, when I mention "the fat red rubber band that comes around the stalks of broccoli" or "the plastic soup containers from the Chinese restaurant" or "mystery screws," there's a lot of guilty laughter. Most of us struggle with throwing these things out. Often people will tell me, "I thought I was the only one!" Yet even if these tendencies are ones you share with others and you can make a case for them, you will need to make some changes in order to live your best life.

A TEST CASE

Let's pretend that you are about to throw out (or put in the recycling bag) a dead flashlight battery, a microwave dinner tray, a stubby candle, a heavy plastic container that once held macaroni salad, and an unopened envelope of coupons. Plus, a bottle of expired vitamins, foam packing peanuts, a cracked flower pot, address labels from your former home, and last summer's L. L. Bean catalog. Picture yourself with the items, and write down in your notebook or here the feelings they evoke in you when you start to toss them.

_____

_____

_____

_____

_____

You may be surprised by your reactions. But maybe not. Near the end of the chapter is a "Dangerous Phrases" sidebar. A *dangerous phrase* is any rationalization that keeps you from taking action. If you don't see something in that list that you wrote down here, there's room to add it.

Family Traditions

"I was saving plastic bags without even realizing why!" my friend Amy told me, laughing. "My mother had a separate pantry closet full of plain brown bags, fancy shopping bags, and hundreds of those flimsy plastic vegetable tear-off bags. I guess I thought that's what you were supposed to do with them. When I gathered everything up to recycle, I heard her telling me, 'You can never have too many bags!' But now I have all this extra space instead, and I'm thrilled."

Household Endangered Species

Often the things you are saving are spares. You'll find some of them, like your old manual typewriter, pictured in the book as "household endangered species." Other spares may include the hard-shell suitcase and the duffel bag with the broken zipper, which were both retired when you bought suitcases with built-in wheels. What about that old VCR player, briefcase, toothbrush, knife set, and pair of hiking boots and the mixer that only works on one speed?

Maybe you have personalized some of them and feel guilty about letting them go, the way you might feel about firing an old retainer if you were an English lord. But remind yourself that they are mass-produced objects that have had a good life (even if they aren't totally dead) and bid them a grateful good-bye. Why should you give them up? Because they are taking up the room you need for other things, and because it is bad feng shui to keep items that are in poor working condition.

Attitude Shifts

Most changes in attitude begin in the mind and then migrate to the emotions and will. When you hear an idea that's contrary to your normal beliefs, your first reaction is to resist it. But you have heard it. The idea has entered your mind, and if it resonates with anything else already there—say, a wish for a better way of living—it will lead you to action. By examining some of your own reasons for holding on, you know where your resistance is coming from. So it's time to consider the following counterbalancing ideas.

Everything Has a Natural Life Cycle

While this is true of people, animals, and plants, it is even more true of stuff. Yet it is not as easy to tell when an inanimate object is dead. Take a box of birthday candles, for example. Say, you buy a box of birthday candles and put them on a cake. By the time the cake is carried to the table, "Happy Birthday" sung, photos taken, and the candles blown out, they are a waxy mess. Someone picks the candles out of the frosting, and the cake gets eaten. The candles have made their contribution; their natural life is over.

But wait! Is that you replacing their remains in the box and slipping the box into a kitchen drawer? Are they going to rest there in their little cardboard coffin, getting in the way of the other things you're trying to locate? Will you take them out periodically but decide they look too shabby for someone else's cake? Well, if they're too worn down for party duty, maybe you can take the bits of saved candles and melt them together, molding and rewicking them to make one large candle. What are the odds of that happening in this lifetime?

Instead, when the party is over, ask yourself, "What is their natural life cycle? Is it over?" Remind yourself that the candles have served their purpose. The rubber band did a good job holding the stalks of asparagus, and the cork helped preserve the wine in the bottle. But the asparagus has been eaten, the wine has been finished, and the bottle is

Household Endangered Species #1
A lock for which no one remembers the combination but that is too good to throw away.

headed for the glass recycling bin. It's time to say good-bye to the helpers. Even if you're sure you can use yet another rubber band for "something." Even if the cork has an interesting imprinted design and you could use it in a collage. If it's that interesting, take a photo.

Buy Fewer but Better-Quality Items

I have been accused of hating cheap umbrellas, but I don't—not really. I even admire the way their sellers can materialize as soon as it begins to rain. But $4 umbrellas are a challenge, because on the first windy day, they turn inside out and you end up with a bent rib or a spoke that has come detached from the fabric. Two or three good storms, and it looks like you are taking shelter under a tulip. This makes the umbrella *imperfectly* good. Better to get temporarily wet than to buy something that will break quickly and leave you with the dilemma of either throwing it out and feeling unhappy or feeling annoyed every time you try to use it.

Better-quality buying of fewer things works for many items, particularly cheap T-shirts that are impulse buys and fade or shrink unevenly as soon as they are washed. You aren't willing to turn them into dustcloths, but you aren't happy wearing them where anyone will see you.

In short, when you consider buying something, don't fall into the trap of justifying, "But it only costs _____."

Recognize That Discarding Something "Perfectly Good" Is Not a Moral Issue

Even though "Waste not, want not" does not come from the Bible—or the Torah or the Koran—the concept of thrift has a religious feeling to it. But even if you believe thrift is a virtue, recognize that there are levels and degrees. Replacing a ten-year-old kitchen because it seems dated or you don't like the color—and sending perfectly good appliances to the landfill—is of greater consequence than tossing that infamous rubber band.

Remind yourself that no one is busily writing down everything you discard. Remind yourself that nobody else *cares*. Based on the way you were raised, you may experience momentary discomfort when you discard an item whose life is over; but once that item is gone, it will be forgotten. In fact, the more often you can find the things you need quickly, the more easily you will be able to say good-bye to the others.

In summation, discarding things that are no longer needed is not a sin. You won't go to hell for throwing away the lower legs of the jeans you made into shorts when the knees wore out. You don't even have to save them to make throw pillows.

Bring Less Home

A good way to avoid the conflict of stuff is to not bring home more than you need. Supermarkets reward customers for buying huge sizes and sometimes give you the second one at half-price. You're actually saving money! But often the savings comes at the cost of spoiled or uneaten food. Can you finish that bushel of peaches before they turn rotten? Can your family be forced to eat that bargain cereal they say they hate? Can you find new uses for a gallon jar of Dijon mustard?

If you're not up to the challenge, don't put yourself in that position just to save a dollar or two.

Seriously Recycle

If discarding items goes against your deeply held beliefs, you can learn how to recycle almost everything. Reuse plastic produce bags or put them in the recycling bins at the store. If you have a yard, get a compost bin and add fruit and vegetable peelings and any uneaten food; then use the results for fertilizer. Shabby towels can go to your local veterinarian; used hearing aids, to Hear Now (800-648-4327). Plastic soup containers and rubber bands from produce can go to a kindergarten teacher to use for mixing paints and other projects. There are many possibilities; we'll discuss them in the last part of this book.

Nobody likes the idea of stuff ending up in landfills. It takes some effort to find alternatives, but do it if conservation is important to you.

Summing Up

To determine if an item is ready to be discarded, you need to look at the object and ask yourself these questions:

- ■ "How is this going to make my life better?"
- ■ "If it were lost in a fire or flood, would I replace it?"
- ■ "Is there a reasonable way to reuse or recycle it?"

If you have no good answer to these questions, it's time to say good-bye. Remind yourself that the item has served its purpose and its life cycle is over. Realize, as well, that no one is going to think you are a bad person or fault you for giving it a decent burial.

DANGEROUS PHRASES

Be on the alert for the following thoughts, which will try and muscle their way in:

- "What if there's another Depression?"
- "I can always use it to _____."
- "But it's still perfectly good!"
- "I'm saving it for spare parts."
- "When I'm off next summer, I'll fix it up."
- "You can't go wrong paying $2 for that!"
- "Waste not, want not."
- "It's a shame to just throw that away."
- "We can always use another one."
- "I'm sure someone could use it."
- "You can never have too many _____."

STUFF LIST #1

Think about the items or groups of items you are holding on to that fall into the categories of "But it's still perfectly good!" and the other dangerous phrases. Then list the items here or in your notebook. For disposition, you have a choice of keep, toss, recycle, give away, or sell.

Item	Why I'm Keeping It	Disposition

When you are struggling to let go of items like these in the future, you can remind yourself:

_____

_____

2

Possession Is Ten-Tenths
of the Law

Years ago, while taking a lunchtime walk with two friends, I spied a carved oak rocking chair that had been discarded by the curb. I love antiques and could tell when I upended the rocker that it was old. Because I was the one who had a place for it, I left my friends guarding the chair and went to get my car. Once I had it home, I sanded and restained several worn areas. The chair looked beautiful.

But after a few years, my decorating style became more eclectic. The rocker, although attractive, wasn't comfortable to sit in, and several of the joints had started to loosen. So I put an ad in the local paper to sell it at a modest price. I had several lookers but no buyers. The rocking chair was shifted upstairs into the guest bedroom.

Why couldn't I let it go? It had literally cost me nothing. I had gotten several years' use from the chair. Although the chair was charming to look at—and useful in creating a cozy, folk-art feeling—its wooden seat and spoked back made it uncomfortable for daily life.

If you want to hear some crazy reasoning, here was mine:

- Even though it had cost me nothing, I felt that the antique rocker was "worth money" and that someone else should pay me for the privilege of owning it next. After all, I had been smart enough to see its potential and rescue it.
- Even though I was sure that if I put the chair outside it would be claimed by one of my neighbors or someone driving by, it seemed like too much of a rejection for the rocker to be placed in the trash twice.
- In *The Little Prince*, Antoine de Saint Exupery writes, "You become responsible, forever, for what you have tamed." In my mind "tamed" had been replaced by "rescued." I had rescued this chair, and its well-being was now my responsibility.

The Endowment Effect

Stuff comes into our lives in many different ways. We buy it, inherit it, find it, are given it as gifts, and so on. But once we have something, it doesn't really matter how it came into our possession; it's ours, just as firmly as if someone had tattooed its image on our wrist. And once something is ours, no matter how we came by the item, giving it up entails a sense of loss.

Social scientists have explained this phenomenon as the endowment effect. In one study, researchers gave half of the participants mugs and the other half the opportunity to buy the mugs from the first group. The mug owners hadn't asked for the cup, hadn't chosen the design, and had paid nothing. Before the study began, they may not have even considered bringing another mug into their lives. Yet once it was theirs, they were reluctant to let it go.

The mugless group was asked to choose the price they would pay for one; the owners, the price at which they would consider selling. On average, the buyers offered $3.50. The sellers wanted about $7.00, so very few exchanges were made. To those who had the mugs, the money had less emotional value than the objects themselves.

There was something else at work here. Besides the feeling of possession engendered by the endowment effect, the underlying principle was that of "loss aversion." The mug owners recognized that giving up the mug—letting it go from their lives—would entail a sense of loss. They were not willing to undergo that without a substantial price to compensate them for the unpleasantness.

It was irrelevant that the mug had cost them nothing and had not even been their choice.

The Personalization of Stuff

Did I really believe the rocking chair had feelings and would suffer shame and rejection if it were discarded by the curb a second time? How embarrassing if I did! But people don't always give their emotions a reality check. We attribute personalities or at least feelings to our cars, stuffed animals, briefcases, favorite bathrobes, dying plants, anything we think might protest when we go to pass it on—especially when it is something that has served us well. I knew that any feelings of regret were all on my part, but it was easier to blame them on the chair.

A Sense of Responsibility

The endowment effect makes us believe that once we have something in our possession, it's ours. But there is an additional reaction to being given something: the idea that once it is ours, its care and fate are in our hands. Adopting a stray kitten who shows up on your doorstep and whom you start feeding is one thing; being unable to throw away a calendar of cute cats and dogs from an animal rescue organization is another.

It may be that, in the case of the calendar, we are transferring our feelings for live animals to their symbols, just as we did as children when we played with dolls or stuffed toys. If someone gives us a plant, whether we like it or not, we feel responsible for keeping it alive. My friend Beth's husband gets upset whenever she wants to uproot a straggly bush in the yard that is way past its prime or discard a houseplant that bears every indication of being deceased. "How can you kill something living?" he asks, incredulous. "If you didn't want to take care of it, you never should have gotten it!"

Ah. As children, we were made to feel responsible for our stuff. How many times did you hear, "If we get it for you, you have to take care of it"? And this was not just in connection with a kitten or puppy, but with a bicycle, a violin, a train set, a delicate watch, a dollhouse, and many other things. We got the message that not only did we have to keep it in good working order but that, as its owner, we were responsible for its fate. It's not unheard of that this role of protector and caretaker extends to anything smaller than ourselves. Even when you toss a plastic angel pin sent to you by a charity, a bell from the past goes off somewhere, and you feel a slight, guilty regret.

The Lure of the Free

When we give up something that came to us for free, we feel that we are not only losing the item itself, we are also losing our advantage.

To wit, say you win an oil painting in a raffle. It may not be something you would buy for yourself, especially if the drawing is based on your ticket stub and not a chance you purchased specifically for the painting. But when your name or number is called, there is the glow of being a winner. You have the (momentary) admiration and envy of everyone else. Maybe your photo is taken. Best of all, you have gotten something of value for nothing!

Later, when you get the painting home, you see it is not really to your taste. You have nowhere to hang it. Yet you can't just throw it away or pass it on.

For one thing, there is the familiar sense of loss when you subtract something from your life. But you are also giving up your special status as a winner. In the case of a curbside find, you are giving away the evidence of yourself as lucky or discerning and ahead of the game. You are forfeiting the right to say, "I found that!" or "I won it!" And who wants to give that up?

Hard-Won Items

Not everything comes to us free. Some things we have to fight for. In those cases, being a winner has a slightly different meaning. Perhaps it is a lamp with a stained-glass shade that catches our fancy at an auction. The bidding becomes heated, and suddenly, owning that lamp is more important to us than anything else. We keep on bidding and finally prevail. Examining the lamp closely, we see it is a little more beat up than it looked on the podium. But it is still beautiful, and even if the cord is frayed, we'll get it fixed. It is ours now for all eternity. If we ever give it away, it will be admitting that it wasn't worth the fight after all.

Sometimes the people we are struggling with are family members. George had made up his mind that the one thing he really wanted from his childhood home was a ship's barometer that had belonged to his great-grandfather, a Nantucket sea captain. Unfortunately, his brother and several cousins wanted it as well. After debating who should have the instrument and not coming to any agreement—his brother turned down a suggestion that they rotate it between their homes—they drew names, and George was the winner. His brother belatedly wanted to rotate it after all. George, to everyone's surprise, agreed with him.

"Relationships are much more important than stuff," he told me. "It seemed silly to let a thing come between us when there was a way to make everybody happy and keep the peace."

Collaterals

It isn't just the things that we win or find that make us feel we are at an advantage. There are the things I think of as collaterals, the by-products that come to us as part of something else. Examples include bubble wrap, stiff cardboard, vinyl containers, fancy hangers, tiny Allen wrenches, jam jars, hotel stationery, loose-leaf binders from seminars, velvet-lined jewelry boxes. Collaterals play supporting roles. But part of their pull for us is that these extras, which we are getting for free, are items that we might otherwise have to pay for. Maybe we have paid for them in the past.

Actually, collaterals can be useful. There's nothing wrong with saving three or four pieces of stiff cardboard if you have occasion to mail out manuscripts or photographs and can use them for backing. The same is true for one or two loose-leaf binders. I usually hold on to one of the little Allen wrenches that come with furniture or picture frame kits, in case the company forgets to include one in the future. But I try to keep the quantities modest.

When you save only what you will actually use, rather than stockpile an entire army, there isn't a problem. The problem comes when everything that crosses your path stays permanently yours.

"It's Genetic"

People like to think that our obsession with our stuff is a recent occurrence, that in the past, Americans lived simpler, more satisfying lives. It is true that many people owned less and thus took better care of what they had—but the emotional connection was just as tight. In 1897 Supreme Court Justice Oliver Wendell Holmes opined in a ruling about property, "A thing which you enjoyed and use as your own . . . whether property or opinion, takes root in your being and cannot be torn away without your resenting the act and trying to defend yourself, however you came by it. The law can ask no better justification than the deepest instincts of man."

But, as I mentioned, the crucial difference is volume. More goods are for sale more cheaply than ever before. Foreign labor and imports, added to the competition of capitalism, have created a plethora of stuff, much more than we need. Unfortunately, there is no built-in genetic wiring that prompts us to say, "No, thanks. I have enough!" We are able to embrace a seemingly inexhaustible amount of stuff, hang on to what is given to us, and accept anything that is free.

"But It Was a Gift!"

Is there anything worse than a gift, especially a hand-crafted one, that you can't stand? Whether it's the rainbow-colored afghan crocheted for you by your aunt, a piece of string art from your best friend of twenty years ago, or a lumpy clay ashtray created by your grandchildren, you can appreciate the thought but not the item. And yet . . .

Consider the fact that Aunt Winnie loves to crochet, your friend made dozens of string pictures when she was into that kind of art, and children are constantly creating things. Perhaps you were just the nearest warm body. Nevertheless, as you dispose of the object, say to yourself, "It was really sweet of _____ to think of me and give me this." This works for purchased gifts as well.

A good alternative to keeping the item is to take a picture of it. Especially in this age of digital photography, it is easy enough to pick up your camera and take a photo of the gift (particularly if it is something handmade) and the giver. Give the giver a copy of the photo as well. This really does soften the blow when the item is not on display after their second visit.

Attitude Shifts

Change starts in the mind and begins with alternative thoughts that you may not have considered. When you first hear these ideas, you may reject them as "wrong." But if you don't dismiss them outright, if you let them take root in your consciousness, they can provide a new perspective. Here are some alternatives to consider.

Household Endangered Species #2
An old family typewriter, still perfectly good, though it needs a ribbon no longer made. It should be saved in case the computer printer breaks down or the country is no longer able to produce electricity.

Easy Come, Easy Go

When you didn't pay for something—it was free or a hand-me-down, won in a raffle, found along the curb, mailed to you from a charity—there is a different dynamic than with something you paid a lot for. Sometimes it's easy to forget that the item cost you nothing financially and that you've already gotten good use from it, if only to make you feel lucky or smart. If it is something you can no longer use or never could, why hang on? Take a photo of it or yourself with it, and move ahead.

If there are any lingering regrets, remind yourself that there will be other gifts from charities, other raffles, better curbside finds.

A Sense of Loss Is Not Inevitable

It's important to remind yourself that every time an item comes into your life, it will be subject to the endowment effect—making it hard to give up. Your automatic response may be a sense of loss, a feeling of diminishment from making your circle of possessions smaller and less varied. But when you know to expect the endowment effect, you realize that it has very little to do with the item itself and not that much more to do with you. Acknowledge that this is human nature and that the more you let things go, the less effect it will have on you emotionally.

After all, you are making your circle of possessions more compact and manageable, more representative of who you are. When you are trying to streamline your life, reducing the quantity of what you own is the fastest way to get there. Remind yourself also that you are gaining a meaningful lifestyle, less hassle, and that vacation house feeling.

Stuff Is Not Alive

When we are small, our parents give us dolls and stuffed toys and encourage us to name them and treat them as if they are alive. On television, locomotives, backpacks, and snowmen talk and sing. The line between what breathes air and what doesn't is blurry to young children. So why wouldn't we carry some half-buried remnant into adulthood and treat our car as if it is a living thing that responds to encouragement and affection? This is a harmless enough practice, except when it affects our ability to discard items no longer useful to us.

One antidote is to picture the assembly lines where cars, teddy bears, briefcases, and other items are turned out by the thousands. They are mass-produced and put together with no thought that they have any individual personality. That comes later from us and can be taken away by us as well.

If you feel hyperresponsible for whatever comes into your life, safeguard what you allow through the door. Don't put yourself in the position of "letting something down."

Some Native Americans do believe that everything has energy or a spirit. If that is how you feel, remind yourself that even if an object seems alive, it doesn't have an active thought process. If you need to, you can explain to the object why you have come to a parting of the ways and that you wish it well.

DANGEROUS PHRASES

Watch out when you look at something and hear yourself say to yourself or someone else any of the following:

- "You'd never know someone had put it in the trash."
- "It doesn't take up that much room."
- "The box is almost as nice as the gift."
- "It didn't cost anything!"
- "It's actually quite nice."
- "I can't give it up now."
- "I've had this _____ forever."
- "I call her Lulabelle."

STUFF LIST #2

Think about the items you are holding on to just because they were free—a raffle prize, something you found along the curb and rescued, a hand-me-down from family or a friend—as well as all the things you're keeping just because they came into your life and now are yours. These include collateral supplies, enticements from charities, items you wrested from other people who wanted them, and anything else for which you feel responsible. Ask yourself these two questions:

- "How is this going to make my life better?"
- "If it were lost in a fire or flood, would I replace it?"

Then list the items here or in your notebook. For disposition, you have a choice of keep, toss, recycle, give away, or sell. Hopefully, many of your outcomes will be to say good-bye.

Item	Why I'm Keeping It	Disposition

_____   _____   _____

_____   _____   _____

_____   _____   _____

_____   _____   _____

_____   _____   _____

_____   _____   _____

_____   _____   _____

   **When you are struggling to let go of items like these in the future,
you can tell yourself:**

_____

_____

Exercise

Once you have filled in the "Disposition" column, you are going
to start using the colored dots you bought. Check your list, and put
a blue dot on any item you plan to give to a specific person (write
that person's name or initials on the dot), a green dot on things for
charity, and a red dot on anything you plan to sell. Toss or recycle
other items right away, and put a yellow dot on anything too large
to put in the garbage. You do not have to "dot" items that you have
decided to keep.

3

A Visit from the Accuracy Police

Imagine this: it is a dark and rainy night, and you hear a knock on the door. Puzzled, you go over and peek out cautiously. Two men in suits and fedoras—the kind worn by Sergeant Joe Friday on "Dragnet" or by FBI agents in old movies—are standing on the threshold. They look official; you let them in.

"We're from the Accuracy Police," the taller one says, showing you his ID. "We need to look at your academic papers."

"But I'm not famous."

"Doesn't matter. You never know."

So you haul out your old textbooks, exams, notebooks, and other papers. Fortunately, you've kept them all.

"Chemistry wasn't your subject, was it?"

"Uh, no."

They move on to your photographs, to make sure you haven't discarded any that are blurry or make you look fat.

Described this way, such a scenario sounds highly improbable. So why do many of us live as if this is what is going to happen?

My father was ready for the Accuracy Police. He had his Eagle Boy Scout Certificate, twenty years of *Marine Engineering* magazines, utility bills back to the 1960s, and all the slides he ever took, including ones that were completely black.

Alas, the inspectors never came, and it was left to my brothers and me to sift through years of stuff.

Most people know they will never receive such a knock on their door. And yet . . .

I suspect my father saved the slides that never came out, miniature black holes, because he didn't want to have to explain why a box that was supposed to have twenty slides only held seventeen. Who knows what kind of subversive plot the Accuracy Police might have accused him of being involved in?

Personal Analysis Time

You're probably thinking that you would never save photos that didn't come out. And I'm sure you wouldn't. But, just for the record, let's take a look at what you may be holding on to.

Very Old Checks, Utility Bills, and Tax Returns

When I asked Mr. Andersen, the husband of a woman who had called me, why he was keeping cartons of paid bills and canceled checks going back to the 1950s, he told me that he wanted a complete financial record. He could not explain it further, and none of my questions could move him beyond that point. If you share Mr. Andersen's sentiments and are unwilling to free yourself from your financial

Household Endangered Species #3
A hammer that will be good as new as soon as you can figure out how to remove the rest of the shaft and buy and install a new one.

burdens, at least mark the cartons clearly so your heirs know that they can be shredded and discarded without being pored over.

Boxes of Unsorted Photographs

Despite the Accuracy Police, photos are not evidence. The only time they rise to that level is when they are taken at a crime scene—though our daily life may be many things, it is not that. But sometimes we have the feeling that it is wrong to discard pictures just because we don't like the way we, or other family members, look in them. We worry that if we keep only flattering photos, our descendants may get the wrong idea about us and think we were more attractive than we are.

Yet good photos are just as representative of you. If you think a picture makes you look like the Michelin Man, if your partner appears dull-witted or your children seedy, rip it up without thinking twice. You *can* throw photos away. Using a digital camera makes it even easier; just push the discard button.

Organizing guides will tell you to throw away photos that are blurry or out of focus, unflattering, boring, failed experiments, or duplicates that you don't plan to give away. This is good advice. But if you have hundreds or even thousands of pictures waiting to be looked at and sorted, I suggest working from the top. Go through quickly and remove the ones you especially like, the ones that make you smile or feel satisfied. Perhaps there will be two or three from a birthday party or vacation that capture the event best. Save these, identify what they are on an acid-free label and stick it on the back, and consider the others fair game to be tossed. The alternative of assessing each photo on its own merit can take weeks, time you may not have or want to spend.

Most photos are taken to document a specific gathering, event, or place. When I recently traveled to Greece, there were a lot of cameras present. Every time a ruin was pointed out to us, everyone—me included—would dutifully photograph it. We took turns photographing each other in front of the remains, perhaps to show we had really been there. More photographs as evidence. Once you lose the sense that you have to keep everything you document, you'll enjoy your photos more.

Cartons of Career Publications, Manuals, and Daily Planners

If you've ever retired from a career or left one job for another, there probably wasn't enough time to get your things in order. Up to the last minute, you were finishing projects, training someone to take over your job, and tying up loose ends. You left after a farewell party, bringing with you a collection of unsorted papers, mugs, and calendars. If it was the end of a long career, you probably already had manuals, printouts, and supplemental texts at home.

At first it seems natural to hold on to everything; it's evidence of how you spent a substantial part of your life. Whether CEO, kindergarten teacher, or the Orkin Man, it's who you were. In any case, it's best to wait a year or so before you face the boxes of old memos, copies of letters, appointment books, corollary materials, company regulations, and student rosters. If some of the supplies aren't too dated, you can offer them to a still-employed colleague. Any confidential business materials should be shredded. Otherwise, give yourself one box for materials you want to keep—commendations, calendars that remind you of interesting experiences, and anything truly memorable. One box, preferably for your entire career, *not* one box per job.

It's also a great idea to have a friend or family member make a short video of you talking about your career—its highlights, what you did, what it meant to you, the people you knew, how you feel about it now. If you've been saving the materials as evidence, the tape will be all you need. It will be interesting to your descendants and makes it easier to resist the urge to hang on to everything.

If you worked in a job with physical materials, the same principles apply. It can be even more of a temptation to keep leftover supplies with the thought that you might want to do something with them. But their presence can keep you from moving on in your life to new activities and interests. After all, you left that position or retired for a reason.

Stacks of Expired Insurance Policies

Most policies run from year to year and are renewed annually, sometimes with minor changes. But when the year is over and the next policy is in effect, the earlier one is history and can be thrown away. The only exception is if you have a claim still pending and need to have the terms in front of you. Otherwise, it is no longer valid and can go.

School Notebooks, Term Papers, and Textbooks

Perhaps this belongs in the chapter on sentimental items—if your algebra textbook still brings tears to your eyes. But most of the time, we hold on to cartons of old school materials with no clear reason why except that they are part of our history. The textbooks are outdated and probably ugly because we underlined or highlighted so many pages, and our class notes aren't much better. What can be worth saving is papers that we wrote that contain original thinking. In going through my parents' things, I was fascinated to come across a paper my mother wrote as an adult when she was completing her degree at Johns Hopkins University. It was like hearing her voice again and reminded me of how smart she was.

The "Certificate of Completion" from Every Seminar You Ever Attended

When I was a social worker for Suffolk County, we frequently were required to attend minicourses or all-day seminars on related topics. These were supposed to help us do a better job, and they often had some value. What didn't have much value was the inevitable certificate we received afterward, proclaiming that we had . . . shown up. Not that we had distinguished ourselves in any way or displayed any brilliance that had been noticed by the presenter—just that we had been there.

I can understand keeping certificates of merit and awards. But I don't know any rationale for holding on to a stack of perfect attendance forms.

Repair Bills for a Car You Don't Own Anymore

You may come across these in a stack of receipts. I found a few going back several years when I was helping Jack reorganize his office. When he glanced at the letterhead and then automatically put them in the "save" pile, I looked at him.

"What? In case the guy I sold the car to has the same problem. He can't accuse me of letting it go and not fixing it."

That made sense. "Did you just sell the car?"

"It was a while ago," he admitted.

"How long?"

"Maybe . . . three years?"

We both started to laugh. "Jack. Even if he came back to you three years later and said the brakes needed replacing, why would you be responsible? Three months, maybe."

"It gets even worse! I didn't sell it to an individual. It was a trade-in." He sighed. "I guess I'm just sentimental about that car."

I glanced down. "Wow. Even when you spent almost two thousand dollars on a new transmission?"

"I did? Forget it!" He discarded the bill immediately.

Greeting Cards from People You No Longer Know

Perhaps you are like the woman who once told me that she had kept every card she had ever received. She didn't mean just personal cards with great sentimental value, but also the miniature calendars from her furnace company, the mimeographed letters from the nice people she had met on a cruise thirty years earlier, and all those elegant cards with nothing but printed names.

If you identify with her, say out loud to yourself, "I'm saving Christmas and birthday cards from people I no longer remember because _____." If you have a good reason, then go for it. Otherwise, say good-bye.

Thirty Years of Secretarial Minutes of the Northwest Area Civic Club That You Inherited as President and Can't Get Anyone Else to Store

Obviously, this refers to any organization you belong to whose records are in your keeping. The materials could be anything from copies of quarterly newsletters going back nineteen years or financial records and treasurer's reports to old membership lists or, of course, the minutes. What makes the situation even stickier is if the organization is now defunct and you have no successor. You can try pawning these things off on your local historical society. Otherwise, contact the other members or former members and see if anyone will take them. If not, explain that you are going to recycle them, and then do it.

Statements of Medical Costs That Were Paid by Your Health Insurance Company

Any chronic illness or hospitalization generates lots of individual costs. If you have good coverage, these will be paid by your insurance company, and you will receive many statements headed "This Is Not a Bill." There is no harm in keeping these for a year or two, to make sure there are no computer errors. But after two years, everything should have been settled, and you can discard the old notices, particularly for things like routine office visits.

Attitude Shifts

I've taken more room than I usually do to lay out the problems, as well as some solutions, in detail. But there are still a few counterbalancing ideas to be considered.

Think of William Morris

When the leader of the Arts and Crafts Movement opined, "Have nothing in your house that is not useful or that you do not believe to be beautiful," he probably did not realize that it would become the motto of the organizing profession. But it is wonderful advice and useful to consider when assessing things.

Most of the items we have been talking about could not be considered beautiful. But are they still useful? If there is no rationale for saving them, don't.

Think of Charles Dickens

Remember how, in A *Christmas Carol*, Ebenezer Scrooge sees the ghost of his old partner, Jacob Marley, dragging long, heavy chains behind him? Jacob tells Ebenezer "I wear the chain I forged in life. . . . I girded it on of my own free will, and of my own free will I wore it." You don't have to take it as far as that, but picture yourself walking around dragging all the cartons of dead storage behind you—old job materials, school books and papers, everything expired, canceled, outdated, vocational materials so boring that no one will ever read them again. You won't get where you want to go tugging all that extra stuff.

Think of Your Descendants

Picture someone else going through all the cartons and boxes and files that you leave behind. The information will mean even less to them, yet they will feel constrained to look at it all. If *you* don't have the time to go through cartons of old textbooks or work memos, why inflict it on anyone else?

Think of William Tell

Or anyone else who represents bravery to you. It does take courage to let go of things when you are holding on to them for security. If you are genuinely fearful of what will happen if you shred your telephone bills from thirty years ago, stop and figure out why. Once you determine the reason, you can move on. It takes bravery to let go of the vague fears, the what-ifs, the "better to be safe than sorry" mentality. But that way of thinking can hold you back from new adventures. The whole point of being brave is to experience life more fully, to follow your bliss.

DANGEROUS PHRASES

- "I'll probably never look at it again, but it's nice to know it's there."
- "I'm keeping it in case I ever get sued."
- "My biographer will need the information."
- "If I ever took another _____ course, I could refer to these notes."
- "It's part of my history."
- "What if someone needs to see it someday?"
- "It shows that I really did _____."
- "It would take years to shred all this!"
- "It's something to look back on in old age."

STUFF LIST #3

Think about all the cartons of old papers and other "evidence" you are holding on to because you have a vague idea that you should. Look back at the items mentioned in "Personal Analysis Time," and list any that you are still holding on to here or in your notebook. Since they are personal items, your choices for disposition would be keep, toss, or shred.

Item	Why I'm Keeping It	Disposition

_____   _____   _____

_____   _____   _____

    When you are struggling to let go of items like these in the future, you can tell yourself:

_____

_____

4

The Information Trap

I was tempted to make this the shortest chapter in the book, simply saying we all have too much paper. Get over it. Or, rather, get rid of it.

But I've been guilty of revering paper, too, especially in the form of books and glossy magazines, and I didn't use the word *trap* in the chapter title lightly. Yet the fact remains that until we accept emotionally that we can never read every newspaper feature, look through every catalog, take advantage of every sale—or find life's deepest answers in the media—we will live in a paper blizzard.

When I ask people in my workshops what their biggest challenge is, the majority call out, "Paper!" So sometimes I suggest that they go through the rooms of their homes and gather it all together—all the newspapers, magazines, flyers, catalogs, coupons, medical journal reports, takeout menus, school notices, outdated invitations, organization newsletters, contest come-ons, playbills, concert programs, brochures about diseases, advertising supplements—and put it in one place: the recycling bag. There are small gasps and then nervous titters when I reassure them that the next day's mail will bring a whole new batch to feed their habit, but that at least they'll be starting from a level playing field.

What is the worst thing that can happen if you go cold turkey and gather and get rid of all the papers just mentioned? Not very much. The catalog companies, charities, and advertisers aren't going to let you go that easily, and if you miss some bit of information, the chances are excellent you'll hear it elsewhere.

Mary, a woman in one of my workshops, sent me an e-mail the week following a workshop where I'd made this suggestion. She remarked, "I did what you said! I actually recycled every old newspaper, magazine, catalog, flyer, and everything else that wasn't crucial. It was scary, but you can't imagine the feeling of lightness and relief I felt afterward when I looked around and every surface was clean! There were no more piles of what I *had* to read haunting me. Since then, I've started sorting the mail at the front door, and most of it doesn't even make it inside."

I can imagine her feeling of lightness and relief. I've seen the same response from other people at the end of a hard decluttering day.

Recycle, Don't File

I'll tell you up front that I don't believe in putting articles and other information in file folders and saving it. Besides the fact that more than 90 percent of what gets filed never gets looked at again, in our age of rapidly changing information, it is already on its way to being obsolete. When I'm writing a book or an article, I'll put pertinent information in a vertical wire holder where I can easily find it. I don't keep anything that I am mildly interested in and feel I might want to write about sometime. Either the urge will pass or it will become more pressing. And if it's the latter, I will need the most current information, which I can almost always find on the Internet.

I overdosed on file cabinets the day I went to Lincoln's house and he took me down in his basement. The walls were completely lined with four-drawer filing cabinets.

"I need you to help me get my files organized," he said.

I went over to one and pulled out a heavy drawer. It was heavy because the papers were so jammed in that nothing could be removed. I spotted untidy sheets of onionskin sticking out, the type that was used years ago to make carbon copies.

"What is this?" I asked.

He shrugged. "Mostly work papers in there. My father's." Lincoln, a handsome, graying school principal, was in his fifties, so I wondered if his father were even still alive.

"What if all this just disappeared? Would you have a meltdown?"

He thought about it. "It would be hard. I like knowing it's here."

"Then leave it. It would be a poor use of our time to spend weeks going through it." But then I thought about why I was there. "What made you call me?"

He chuckled. "Well, I'd thought about moving down south when I retire next year. I have a lot of family there, and I've gotten to hate these winters. But a moving man told me it would cost a fortune to move all of these, and I wouldn't have a place for them anyway."

I laughed, too. "And you hoped I could make half of them magically disappear. I can, but . . . Look, when you're ready to move, call me and I'll help you clean them out. But I won't go through them paper by paper."

He looked crestfallen.

"When you retire next year, why don't you rent a place near your family and start spending time there? If you really enjoy it—without this ballast—then it will make it easier to dispose of it."

He smiled. "I like that idea."

So What Do I Do with It?

I can hear you right now saying, "But what about . . ."

Yes, there are papers we all have to keep: birth and marriage certificates, passports, vehicle titles, mortgages and leases, military discharge papers, adoption records, divorce papers, and so on. These should be in a safety deposit box or a secure drawer. Then there are other papers that are personally important to us to save. But none of them deserve to be shut up in a file cabinet, never again to see the light of day.

File Cabinet Alternatives

Statistically speaking, almost all material that gets shut away in a file cabinet never gets looked at again. To keep that from happening, I find that the following alternative storage options work best.

A Memorabilia Box. This is a sturdy cardboard box with a separate lid, about thirty inches long, fifteen inches wide, and fifteen inches high. You can find them at IKEA and stationery suppliers. My husband, Tom, and I each have one. They hold old letters, awards, diaries, special cards, school papers, kids' art, and so on. New things get laid on the top, and about once a year, I go through mine and remove what no longer seems meaningful. Everything I'm saving from the past (except for photographs) is in this one place.

A Hope Chest. Smaller in size, this box can hold recipes you want to try, travel brochures, craft ideas, holiday magazine ideas, woodworking plans, gift ideas, and pages from magazines or catalogs that you find inspirational. In short, anything you see that makes you think, "I'd like to do this/go there/try that." Since you only have one box, when it starts to get full, you'll need to carefully purge what no longer seems as appealing. You can put the items in clear plastic sleeves (eight and a half by eleven inches) to protect them and make things easier to locate. I don't have a hope chest right now—not because I have no hope, but because my ideas are in my head, with the Internet as my source.

When I did have a hope chest, I liked the fact that the box was portable and I could sit comfortably and look through it. It also kept all my ideas in one place, easily accessible.

A Bill and Receipts Drawer. When your bills and monthly statements come in, they should go immediately to one section of a drawer where you also have stamps and envelopes. In the back of the same drawer you can put your monthly bank statements, receipts for taxes, and credit card statements so that they'll all be together at income tax time. You don't need to save those little tear-offs that say, "Save this portion for your records." I pay my bills on the Internet now, but I still keep the drawer for one-time invoices and forms I need to complete.

A Standing Paper Holder. This vertical file can be placed on your desk or in a deep drawer. In the sections of my file I keep a folder with details on upcoming speaking engagements, travel information, and invitations. Another folder has projects I'm currently working on. A third has crucial information that I need to be able to find in a hurry. And so on. That's it. My friend Terry, a children's educational writer who works at home, swears by a rolling file cart that keeps all her projects within view.

But It's a Book!

Most of the books we hold on to are kept, not because we need to refer to them, but because they are books. As the title of an Anthony Powell novel indicates, "books do furnish a room." They are colorful, and they hint at adventure and knowledge, as well as our intelligence in having so many. There are people who would say that you can never have too many books; certainly, piles of them are more acceptable than stacks of last year's newspapers. When I hear that someone has a personal library of ten thousand books, I feel a surge of admiration.

That said, I still think there is great potential for inappropriately holding on to books. Some of the main reasons for parting company are detailed in the sidebar "The Top Ten Reasons to Let a Book Go." In Step 3 I'll discuss in detail the options you have for finding new homes for books. But plan to go through your shelves and cartons carefully. Books past their prime can bog you down and keep you from new adventures.

THE TOP TEN REASONS TO LET A BOOK GO

1. You couldn't get into it. How often do you buy a book because it looks interesting or it won the National Book Award or a friend raved about it? Sometimes you get it as a gift. Unfortunately, you can't get past the first chapter. Still, you hold on to it, thinking something will change. Since it won't be the book, it will have to be you.

2. You enjoyed the book, but you know you'll never read it again. It's time to pass it on to a friend or your local library.

3. Your interests have changed. A subject you were passionate about five or ten years ago is no longer on the radar. So when you look at the book and it seems like past history, it is.

4. The information is outdated. Older cookbooks with fat-laden recipes are not the kind you're interested in right now. Other books that get quickly outdated are travel guides, almanacs, medical guides, textbooks, encyclopedias, computer how-tos, and books relating to any other field where the information is changing quickly. They aren't old enough to be antiques or even quaint; they're just misguided.

5. The book is attractive but too general. You know the kind: books covering the complete history of music, dolls, archaeology, Western art, the world, and so on. Because the book tries to be so comprehensive, you'll find little detailed or valuable information once you've skimmed its pages.

6. You mistakenly think the book is valuable. The trouble with classics printed a hundred or more years ago is that, unless they are first editions, they have little monetary value. Most of them were published as a volume in the collected works of a particular author. What books are valuable? Signed first editions of vintage fiction, some specific art books, illustrated classics with small print runs, and so on. If you want to know the value of a particular book, check out what it is selling for on abebooks.com or eBay.

7. The book is falling apart physically. Loose bindings where chunks are falling out, yellowed or crumbling pages, a hard-to-read typeface—all are indications that the volume is past its prime.

8. You don't have room to display your books without looking cluttered. That means it's time to let go of all the volumes you don't care about; you can't love them all equally.

9. The best thing about the book is that it's inscribed to you. Anything personalized is harder to get rid of, and books are no exception. But if you don't know the author personally and won't read the book again, let it go.

10. You don't love it. When you look at a pleasure book—as opposed to one you're keeping for reference—there should be a chemical reaction, a frisson of feeling. If such a book doesn't make you feel good, it has outlived its place.

Attitude Shifts

In order to loosen the hold that paper may have over your life, here are some counterbalancing ideas.

It's Not Necessary to Read Everything

According to the U.S. Postal Service, approximately ten billion catalogs were mailed in 2005. Add to that more than ten thousand magazines and journals, not to mention daily and weekly newspapers, advertising circulars, brochures in doctors' offices, and so on. Much of the information they contain is repeated from venue to venue.

Even if you only feel responsible for reading what crosses your path, that can be much too much. If you know you have a compulsion to save paper until you've read every word, be very careful what you let through the door. Sort your mail outside over a recycling bin, and remind yourself that 95 percent of what comes to you in the mail—catalogs, solicitations from charities, advertising flyers, magazine subscription offers, coupons, free newspapers, and so on—just wants your money. Don't consider these harmless; at best, they are like a persistent salesperson selling magazine subscriptions "for a good cause." Once they get a foot in the door (or a spot on your kitchen counter or dining room table) they will hang around until you give in.

You Don't Need to Keep Other People Informed

Sometimes people feel it is their duty not only to go through everything to keep up for themselves, but to clip out helpful information for family or friends. Initially, your underlying fear is that if you don't look at everything, you might miss that one crucial piece of information that will make you richer, smarter, or better at relationships or that may even save your life! But then you start worrying about other people and begin clipping items for them as well. I understand the impulse. Once in a while I'll read something and worry for a moment about my little grandchildren. But I

Household Endangered Species #4
No one is really sure what it is or where it came from, but it's been in the family forever.

also know that if it were anything significant, their parents would hear about it.

If It's Not Important Enough to Read Right Away, It Will Never Be

When something significant catches your attention in a newspaper or on a magazine cover, you either turn to it and read the item right away or leave it open so you can get back to it as soon as possible. Most magazines you subscribe to have one or two articles like that per issue, as well as, perhaps, a column you always read. After you look at those, you put the magazine aside to read the rest later. But later rarely comes. There are newspapers with compelling articles of their own, phone calls to make, TV programs to watch. Life comes rushing in, bringing newer and more interesting information, and the material you were not interested in enough to read right away becomes a stacked-up obligation.

Just for a month, try this: when a newspaper, magazine, or catalog arrives, take the time to go through it and read or look at anything you're vitally interested in. Once you've done that, put it in the recycling bag. It may feel awkward and uncomfortable at first, but at the end of the month, see how uncluttered things are. You may think, "What's the point of having a subscription if I only read one or two things?" Hold that thought—at least until the publication comes up for renewal.

Consider That Information Can Be an Addiction like Any Other

Practice saying aloud, "My name is _____, and I'm a paper junkie." Just kidding. But my friend Adele wisely won't subscribe to the daily paper because she knows she would spend hours reading it. Tom has the paper as his home page online. I like looking at the physical paper the first thing in the morning, with coffee and cuddly cats, but I'm too anxious to start the day to get bogged down in reading stories that don't seem immediately fascinating. At the end of the day, it goes in the recycling bag.

The point is, if you are compelled to read every word and have a problem with newspapers, magazines, and catalogs piling up, admit that you have a compulsion and lock the door. Cancel whatever you can.

OUTFOXING THE PAPER MONSTER

- Don't automatically renew magazine subscriptions.
- Don't bring home concert programs, playbills, church bulletins, and other event detritus. It's just as easy to leave these on a chair on your way out.
- Don't fall into the temptation of buying a pamphlet or guidebook on your way through the gift shop of a historical home, museum, or monument after your tour. If you don't read it in the first hour afterward, you never will—and just how likely is it that you will read it an hour after your tour?
- Don't put your name on a mailing list to receive free newsletters, notices, or updates.
- Don't let newspapers accumulate when you're on vacation, with the thought that you'll catch up on your reading when you get home. Suspend delivery when you're gone. You'll be busy enough catching up with everything else when you return.
- Don't bring home materials from a seminar or workshop unless you know you'll lose your job if you don't.
- Don't say, "I'll take them!" when someone offers ten years of *Gourmet* magazine.

Remind Yourself "I'd Rather Be _____ *"*
When you think about it objectively, there may be other things you'd
rather be doing than spending hours trolling for information in the
magazines, newspapers, and brochures that you've accumulated. The
trouble is, the material is right there, and the other things require
more effort—whether going for a bike ride, creating a work of art,
working in the garden, or visiting with a friend. If you ask yourself,
"What is the best use of my time right now?" the best answer may
not be "Thumbing through some old catalogs to make sure I haven't
missed something."

DANGEROUS PHRASES

- "I haven't read it yet!"
- "I'm saving it to read on vacation."
- "The things it advertises aren't sold in stores."
- "As long as I subscribe to it, I may as well read it."
- "It has great photographs!"
- "I need to warn my children about this disease."
- "But it might be something important!"
- "This item may never be offered again."
- "I like to keep up with what's going on."
- "I know it's here somewhere. I just read it last week!"

STUFF LIST #4

If you are living in a paper blizzard, think about everything that you bring home or are saving to read. Then list each category here or in your notebook. Books have a separate exercise at the end of the chapter.

Item	Why I'm Keeping It	Disposition

When you are struggling to let go of items like these in the future, you can tell yourself:

_____

_____

Exercise

Go through the books on your shelves as well as the ones heaped in piles. Have your colored dots at hand. Look at each book and notice whether you have (1) an emotional pull toward it and the desire to read it again, (2) the sense that you will need to refer to it for information, or (3) the feeling that having it in your life makes you happy. If you experience such feelings with a particular book, you may want to keep it. If not, use the dot system: blue dots (with name of intended recipient) for books to give away, green dots for those going to charity, and red dots for those to be sold.

Don't put any dots on the books you are keeping. Simply throw away those that are outdated (see the sidebar on page 52). You can leave the books with dots on the shelves or in stacks for now and start giving away the blue-dotted ones when you see the people for whom they are intended.

As far as any books you've been keeping in cartons, unless they are new purchases, recognize that they are already halfway out the door and help them the rest of the way.

5

"I'm Getting Sentimental Over You . . . and You . . . and You"

When I discuss sentimentality in my workshops, I point out that most objects, no matter how beloved they once were, have a shelf life. Souvenirs and memorabilia that thrilled us a few years earlier gradually lose their power and are replaced by something different.

Leonore came up to me at the end of a program. "But what if you still love everything? I feel an emotional connection to everything I have!"

I smiled. "Can you fit it all in your memorabilia box?"

"One box? I don't think so! My things from camp alone take up several boxes."

"What kind of things?"

"Oh, you know. The crafts I made, my skit costumes, my awards, the clothes I wore, letters we exchanged during the year. We had our thirtieth reunion, and people couldn't believe that I still had everything!"

"It sounds like camp was one of the high points of your life."

"It was! I went to the same camp from when I was eight to when I was a counselor. But it wasn't the only high point. I still have every outfit my boys ever wore and all their toys."

I was beginning to get the picture, and it was one that many people would run screaming from. But evidently not Leonore. "Is there a problem?" I asked.

"Just that I'm running out of room," she confessed. "And at a time I should be thinking about moving to a *smaller* place."

We arranged a consultation for the following week. Leonore didn't want it at her house, so we met at a quiet spot for coffee. As we talked, I learned that her sons were grown and her husband had moved out two years before and was getting remarried.

"So what are your future plans?" I asked. "What do you look forward to doing next?"

"Oh, I don't know," she said vaguely. "Wait till my sons get married and I have grandchildren, I guess."

"Oh, come on," I said. "You're too young to give up on life! But you have to deal with the past first. Once you can look ahead, we can work with your things."

Leonore went back to a therapist she had seen in the past and a year later called me. "I'm ready!" she said. By then she was working with a children's theater group and had a list of places to which she planned to travel. She had regained her zest for life. She saved her wedding album for her sons but gave up most of her mementos from her failed marriage, as well as the boxes and boxes of old children's clothing and toys. By separating out the things that were emotionally important to her from a lot of things that weren't, she was able to get things down to two memorabilia boxes—all that she had room for in her new life.

Stopping Time

Now we come to one of the hard parts that Leonore faced. In *Cleaning and the Meaning of Life*, Paula Jhung talks about the problem she had with her children's clothes. "I saved so much of my kids' apparel that I could have opened a baby boutique. It wasn't just because those tiny smocked dresses and embroidered bibs were so cute, it was because it was hard to see my girls grow up. Once I figured that saving their things wasn't going to slow the process, I could finally give it all away."

Even though your children are grown, you may still be holding on to that four-bicycle car rack, hockey sticks, and camping equipment. Although you know you will never sleep in a tent again or use that blackened cooking set, you had many happy family vacations with them. In your heart you know that particular stage of life is over, but still . . .

One thing you can do is celebrate it. Enlarge a photo of your family on a camping trip and put it in a visible spot. The idea of "We *did* it—that was us" can release you from holding on and help you give away obsolete equipment. There's a whole world of adventure still waiting for you out there.

Perhaps you were a daredevil downhill skier or scuba diver or crack marksman, but over time your physical abilities or interests have waned. There's no rationale to keeping clunky equipment around to remind you of your glory days. Again, take a photo or have an older one (with you participating in the activity) enlarged.

If you're hanging on to any old uniforms—from army fatigues to a cheerleader's outfit, a stained football jersey, or a dentist's white coat—ask yourself what your reasons are. Then ask yourself if a photograph could do as well. You will be surprised at the answers.

I don't mean to suggest that holding on to sentimental items is limited to golden agers. I've worked with people in their twenties who were buried in stuffed animal collections or sports memorabilia from their high school days and young parents who felt they should save every nursery school painting. Although the first forty years of life are generally a time of amassing the stuff that you will spend the next forty years trying to get rid of, you can get just as cluttered and bogged down sooner if you don't start making choices. It is not just a matter of whether you have room for your past but also of what impact your past is having on your present.

The Power of the Past

Although America's past is recent compared with many other countries, we are enthralled by our history. We love to visit old battlefields, historic homes, Boot Hill cemeteries, and museums—to say nothing of antique shops, eBay, and "Antiques Roadshow." We love to live in old houses that have stories embedded in their walls. When we buy antiques it is not only because they are beautiful but also because they are burnished with romance. An eighteenth-century cup may promise to enhance your life, though your imagination has to do the actual work.

I am as susceptible to the lure of antiques as anyone else and am happy to supply a history for them. But over the years I've learned several things. For one, I don't have to actually *own* the object; I can appreciate it at Monticello or the Metropolitan Museum of Art without having to become its caretaker. For another, since it is not part of my current culture, there's a danger in surrounding myself with so many anachronisms that I'm not living in the present. Finally, even the most appealing inanimate object is just that—inanimate. It will never love you back.

Protecting the Elderly

Sometimes we aren't only sentimental about obsolete equipment—we also feel we need to protect it, to keep it from becoming extinct. Has it survived all these years only to be junked by us? If we don't keep its memory alive, who will? These things have an innocence that appeals to us. A treadle sewing machine, a hand-cranked ice cream maker, a rusted tractor, and a blackened kerosene lantern all speak of a less frenzied, more peaceful time. When we find one of these items in its native habitat—a cellar, barn, or shed—we're as delighted as any archaeologist. We wouldn't dream of discarding it!

Having a few links with the past is wonderful, but it's a slippery slope. You find a Hoosier cabinet at a country auction, and the next step is to fill it with pottery bowls, utensils, and colorful tins from its original period. While charming, it's a very large collectible in a kitchen that probably needs the room for your present life. You can do even less decorating with an obsolete piece of machinery.

To set your mind at ease about throwing away the last of its kind, visit the Henry Ford Museum in Dearborn, Michigan, or the Smithsonian Institution in Washington, D.C. They make a practice of saving such items in all their variations.

Living in the Past

Decorating with period furniture and antiques can evoke a nostalgia for what we imagine as a warmer, more authentic time. We imagine that relationships were warmer, values sounder, and neighbors more neighborly. By decorating our rooms this way, we are tapping into this preferable past. But since the objects of a hundred years ago don't have a direct connection with our lives, in themselves they lack the ability to re-create the idealized life we're hoping for. We're the ones who have to do the work.

Sometimes period decorating can be like completing a puzzle or creating a piece of art, a treasure hunt in which we research and track down the pieces and put them all together to create something new. Or, in this case, something old. There's a delicate balance between having things around you that create the spirit of another time and living in the past, but with the right balance it's very rewarding. While I never wish I had been born in another century—I'm too fascinated by the world right now—I love having some things that reach backward and reflect where we came from.

"It's Too Cute to Throw Away!"

There are whole categories of items that our culture tells us we should respond to positively, from angels to toddlers. What kind of hard-hearted person can toss out a calendar filled with photos of adorable kittens that came from an animal charity? Not many—at least, not right away.

First, the calendar has to be added to the stack on the kitchen counter or dining room table, glanced through and admired, then placed on another pile. Finally, it makes it to the desk, where the two cutest pictures are removed (for framing, making cards, or sending to a friend) before it hits the recycling bag. And the fate of the two saved pictures? You don't want to know. But they are in good company. Lots of company. And this mostly because we have been conditioned to feel sentimental when we see something small, warm, and fuzzy, with a cute face.

The point is, you need to distinguish between what honestly moves you and what the world is telling you should melt your heart. If something doesn't reach you on a personal level, let it go. It's hard enough dealing with everything that does.

Future Nostalgia

Is it possible to feel nostalgic for things you haven't actually done? It is when you feel sentimental about an image of yourself that you have held on to for years, even if you haven't put it into action yet. Some of these statements may sound familiar to you:

- "I always wanted to _____."
- "My plan was to visit _____."
- "I always imagined myself doing _____."

But something happened, and although you collected material about whatever your dream was, you never actually did it. You may have moved on to other things but saved the information or the equipment or the supplies. And even though you are still no closer to doing whatever it is and, in some cases, the time to do it is over, you don't feel able to close the door on what might have been. Relinquishing the dreams of your younger self seems just too hard.

"Where there's life, there's hope," you tell me, looking at the scraps of cloth that haven't been made into a quilt or the in-line skates still in the box or the brochure about getting an M.F.A.

I agree and tell you that you have three choices: (1) you can set a deadline for when you'll start making it or taking steps toward doing whatever it is, (2) you can put as much of it as will fit into your hope chest, or (3) you can decide that too many past hopes are weighing you down and let it go.

When you choose the third option, you may feel some momentary regret and then a sense of freedom that you can focus on something else. Once that particular hope is relinquished, you can look for new dreams with a fresh enthusiasm.

The Antisentimental

People sometimes hold on to things that made them unhappy, either because it is part of their history or because they are not yet ready to deal with them. Once in a while it is because things have become so familiar that these people no longer even *see* them. In Chapter 3, I talked about how to handle the personal papers you are saving because they have "historical value." If some of what you feel sentimental about falls into this category, go back to that chapter and look at what your options are.

Household Endangered Species #5
A large collection of stuffed animals that feels as if it is part of the family and would be crushed if you gave it away.

The second reason for holding on to certain items is that

they are painful to revisit but need to be dealt with. Sheila, the survivor of a difficult divorce, has paper bags full of materials, both legal and personal, that she needs to go through. "But I can't stand seeing anything that even has his handwriting on it," she says bitterly. "I get upset all over again."

This is the time it is good to have a friend or sympathetic family member help you. In Sheila's case, that person would not necessarily have to go through the papers with her but could just be there to talk and laugh and let her vent her frustrations or cry. Having another person on your side at a time like this can give you a sense of support. I don't advocate the plan of doing a little each night. It's better to yank out a sore tooth with one quick, if painful, action rather than prolong the agony over weeks.

What about letting go of letters, photos, and mementos from a significant relationship that is now over, when the parting was amicable? Even in this case, if you're looking for someone new, it's better to keep only a few things and let the others go. They may be hidden away, but *you* know they're still there, telling your subconscious that you're not ready for another relationship. Remember, you're keeping only what can fit in one memorabilia box.

Inherited Sentimentality

Sooner or later most of us end up having to go through the households or belongings of deceased family members. This is something I had to do several times within a five-year period. At first it seems disrespectful to give away any of the items. They represent the belongings of someone we loved. But gradually we realize that the person wasn't equally attached to all of them. Think about your pots and pans, linens, appliances, furniture, and clothing. Would you want your children or younger relatives to feel that they had to keep them all and incorporate them into their lives? Or would you be happy to see such items go to someone truly in need who could get some use from them?

There will be photographs, family heirlooms, valuable collections, and beloved objects that are in a different category and should be divided among you and your siblings or cousins. But the sooner you can get over the idea that all family belongings are sacrosanct and can find good homes for the large majority of them, the better you will feel. As it is, you will bring home more things than you need and will have to let go of them gradually. It takes time to mourn your loss and to emotionally separate the person from his or her things.

Attitude Shifts

To stop yourself from regularly succumbing to sentimentality, try the following counterbalancing measures.

Sentimental Objects Don't Last Forever

You can see examples of this in your own life. You bring back a souvenir from a memorable vacation, certain that it will always remind you of your wonderful time. At first, it does. But after five years, the link becomes fainter. In ten years, you look at the souvenir and feel nothing at all. If it's something you use, like a bowl or pitcher, it has another purpose. But if it's simply decorative, its time is up.

To continue on the topic of vacation souvenirs, you purchase them in a place you are enthralled by, believing that the object will have the same magic. On my first trip to Santa Fe years ago, I fell in love with the Southwest and brought home a chile ristra as big as a toddler. I hung it on the door of my Cape Cod house, where a mass of chile peppers looked a little strange, though I was too infatuated to notice. Unfortunately, the humid Long Island air made quick work of them.

Vacation souvenirs can quickly become household endangered species. You thought that the little boy passing water into the fountain, one of the main attractions of Brussels, was adorable and funny. But the replica you brought home soon seems tasteless. Or you bought a little "weather house"—with the figures that pop out when rain is predicted—in Switzerland or a miniature cannon at Gettysburg or an Italian tapestry of da Vinci's *Last Supper*. Things that seemed inspiring in their place of origin can seem silly in your home.

A vacation souvenir might not even be something you buy. Rocks have beautiful colors under water, and driftwood and shells on the beach are picturesque. But things in nature look best in their natural habitat; once out of it, they seem to lose their glow.

Staying in the Moment Is the Most Satisfying Way to Live

If life is like a mountain railroad, it's natural to want to walk up to the front car once in a while and see where you are headed—as well as to make sure you are still on the right train. But most of the time, you are looking out the window, enjoying the passing scenery, and staying in the moment where the action is. It's not very satisfying to spend your time in the rear car, looking out at what you've already passed.

It's a form of living in the past to rely on the memory of bygone events to give us a jolt of happiness. We all do it at times, and it adds to the richness of life. But when people tell me, as someone inevitably does, that they "feel sentimental about everything," it makes me think they either have not taken the time to sort through their memorabilia or are not getting much pleasure from their current lives. If you are caught up in what you are doing, living fully every day, it doesn't leave much time for reminiscing.

Sometimes people who do live in the present nevertheless have the image of themselves sitting around reliving the past when they are "old." But does this happen? When is "old" old enough to stop looking for new adventures? I was in line at a garden shop when the man ahead of me (he was buying a refill canister for a gas grill) announced gleefully to the cashier that he had turned one hundred the week before. Awed, I watched him heft the cylinder. It didn't seem like he was on his way home to read some old Christmas cards.

Put Away the Umbrella

So if you're hanging on to things in anticipation of the "rainy day" of old age, realize that if you're fortunate, it will never come. The line between retirement and the remainder of life has become blurred; people are increasingly pursuing part-time work and new passions and living in the moment. Holding on to boxes of things that you don't have time to look at now but are sure you will someday may just be a mirage.

You can live in the present, savoring each moment, for your entire life.

Think about that wonderful vacation trip again, from a new perspective. When you travel, you don't have your familiar stuff around you. But it doesn't matter. You are so involved in the new experiences you are having, the new sensations, that you don't give much thought to the things you currently own or your past experiences. Why shouldn't your daily life be as exciting?

DANGEROUS PHRASES

- "I'm saving everything so my children can decide what they want."
- "Call me sentimental, but . . ."
- "Something this old has to be valuable."
- "I've never seen one like it!"
- "Those dishcloths were given to my mother when she got married."
- "They don't even make these anymore."
- "Life was so much better then!"
- "This is the can from the first beer I ever drank."

STUFF LIST #5

Look around you at all the items you have that serve—or used to serve—a sentimental purpose, either because you were told that you should save them to commemorate an occasion or because they are cute. Think about things you are keeping because they are obsolete or antique, the souvenirs you thought would be meaningful forever. Include items to which you are still attached. Then list the items here or in your notebook. For disposition, you have a choice of keep, toss, recycle, give away, or sell.

Item	Why I'm Keeping It	Disposition
_____	_____	_____
_____	_____	_____
_____	_____	_____
_____	_____	_____
_____	_____	_____
_____	_____	_____
_____	_____	_____
_____	_____	_____
_____	_____	_____
_____	_____	_____
_____	_____	_____

_____   _____   _____   _____

_____   _____   _____   _____

_____   _____   _____   _____

   When you are struggling to let go of items like these in the future, you can tell yourself:

_____

_____

Exercise

Once you have filled in the "Disposition" column, use the dot system (described at the end of Chapter 2) to indicate where items are going.

6

Creating the Good Life

When I was first out of college, I worked for a religious magazine in Philadelphia. One night we were all invited to the editor's home for a barbecue. While the men were kibitzing around the grill, the editor's wife took the rest of us on a tour of their impressive home. As we admired her state-of-the-art appliances, she said, "Yes, I'm so thankful God gave me this wonderful kitchen to cook in!" As we returned to the yard, she added, "I think God gave us this beautiful home to serve as an example to others."

People talked like that then. As I pondered it on the way back to my rented apartment, the message became clear. If you're a good enough person, you'll be rewarded with a high standard of living.

The Life List

Perhaps it would be easier if we were given a printed list of expectations and the specific items we should own at each stage of our lives. Despite extensive advertising, we muddle along buying stuff that we feel we are supposed to have, hoping we are getting it right.

The sense of having to be on task at every phase of life is reinforced by what we see on television. In both the advertisements and programming, we are shown the kind of home we *should* be living in based on our age and background, the way we should look, the car we are expected to drive, the things we should own. Much of the message is subliminal; we are absorbing these values during commercials for cereal or vitamins or wall paint. The people shown are doing slightly better than we are, but we could catch up to them if only we used these products and a few others.

If you can say to yourself, "At my age I should have," and not have an immediate list come to mind, you're in the minority.

The March of Progress

Built into our lives is the idea that we are on our way to somewhere else and have to show progress. Schools are set up so that we get promoted every year. Most companies and organizations start new employees at entry-level jobs and give them a professional ladder to climb. So it is probably no surprise that many people believe they should show progress in their possessions. How else will we know how we are doing?

Buying to Keep Up

Jane Hammerslough, the author of *Dematerializing*, points out that "the threat of social retribution for failing to live up to certain material standards has lurked for a long time" and then describes a 1930 magazine ad for a particular kind of toilet seat. In it a young woman overhears her tea party guests whispering about the shortcomings of her bathroom. Shocked, she realizes exactly what the problem is and vows to change it immediately.

These days, keeping up is more complicated than buying a bathroom accessory. We sometimes feel as if we are surrounded by the equivalent of those gossiping ladies who are watching to see the kind of car we drive, where we vacation, and, depending on our reference group, whether we wear clothes from Ralph Lauren or Geoffrey

Beene or L. L. Bean. You may feel that if you don't, you'll be thought of as "not doing that well" or "not really one of us."

Promises, Promises

It is the nature of advertising to imbue objects with supernatural powers. A particular set of golf clubs recommended by Jack Nicklaus will make you a better player. A set of expensive French cookware will turn you into a dazzling chef. The most innovative DVDs for toddlers are necessary if you want them to get into a good college. Giving your wife a large diamond ring will show the world not only that you've made it big but that you have the perfect relationship.

But what happens when the promises don't materialize, when your golf game or your cooking doesn't dramatically improve, and rubies, not diamonds, turn out to be the stone of the year? You don't get rid of any of your purchases. You just look for something better, something more, that will do what it is supposed to. In a year or two, it will be something else. I just read an article that tipped me off that large Sub-Zero refrigerators are now being replaced by under-the-counter styles designed to conceal the fact that they are refrigerators at all.

It is no accident that companies pay celebrities handsomely to endorse their products. It is not that using the same product as an Olympic gold medalist will make you as good an athlete exactly, but the promise is nevertheless there. Also, the fact that something is identified with someone famous means that, when you use it, you are identified with him, too, and know him in a way. The item will hold a special promise for you as long as you keep that aura alive in your mind.

The Props We Need

Buying items that we feel we need is a little different than bringing home new stuff for the thrill of it. In order to play the role you see yourself in, whether it be seasoned intellectual, successful attorney, or stay-at-home mom, you feel you need external evidence so that other people can identify you. This is a kind of shorthand that has its uses, though sometimes it can lead to disastrous negative profiling.

For our purposes, the problem comes when we are unable to discard our outworn props and instead hang on to everything, old and new.

How Things Accumulate

And that is one way things accumulate. When you buy an expensive shampoo that promises gorgeous hair, you tend to keep it even when the results are disappointing. Maybe your hair is the problem, and the shampoo will work better next week. When you try to keep up with what you are supposed to have at a particular age, everything else you have bought up until that time doesn't just dissipate. The man who bought his wife a large diamond and then found he now needs to get her a ruby as well doesn't ask for the diamond back for a trade-in.

So sports equipment and tablecloths and sweaters and exotic cookware and outdoor grills and cell phones and computer programs and hundreds of other things accumulate because the one that has been replaced is still perfectly good. Things that don't have a chance to wear out before they are replaced tend to hang around, especially when they are subject to the "I paid good money for this!" rationale. Since you were once satisfied with them, it's always possible that you will be again. So you keep them, just in case.

Lateral Multiplication

In order to live the good life, you often need to buy things that come with a supporting cast of thousands. Cookware is a good example. You can create a wonderful meal with fresh ingredients, one or two pots, a frying pan, and a sharp knife. Yet when you look in any instructional cookbook, you'll find pages of "necessary equipment." This equipment includes special pans, assorted knives, deboning tools, food mills, mortars and pestles, a collection of exotic staples, and some other things that you probably haven't even heard of before.

What happens when a busy young couple decides to get married and is suddenly plunged into a world of Waterford candlesticks and sterling pickle forks? Since items that used to be wedding gifts are now given at showers, the pair is sometimes at a loss as to what to request on a gift registry. Store lists are filled with items such as juice extractors, ricers, sushi makers, bread machines, chafing dishes, and meat slicers, to say nothing of smaller items, like zesters, melon ballers, and garlic presses.

In a *New York Times* article, Gretchen Rubin represents many brides when she confesses, "I fell right into the trap of aspirational registering—signing up for things that I imagined I'd need if I were the kind of elegant, sophisticated person I wished I were. So we received several presents that terrified me. I only started using the white linen place mats last year."

The idea of white linen place mats *is* terrifying. Even if you eliminate red wine, juicy meat, blueberries, chocolate, and half of everyone's favorite foods, the placemats will still need to be prepped, washed, and ironed after each use. Many things like that get kept but are never used because they are impractical and labor-intensive. Copper-bottomed pots look beautiful and impressive hanging in your kitchen, but it's hard work to keep them shiny. When cooking, we end up using the same few workhorses instead.

Household Endangered Species #6
A collection of all the holiday cards you have received over the years, which you plan on putting into albums.

Attitude Shifts

These principles of multiplication and escalation are good

reasons to get off the stuff merry-go-round, but there are other reasons that make even more sense.

Our Possessions Are Subject to the Law of Diminishing Returns

There are a few things that we buy, inherit, create, or are given with which our bond becomes stronger over time. But for each of those there are ten others that we lose interest in when their novelty wears off. The reason for this is known as the process of adaptation. What was exciting in the beginning turns into something we are accustomed to, something we derive less pleasure from. Repeated exposure diminishes our return. If we aren't careful, we will go out and try to recapture the excitement by buying something new.

In *The Paradox of Choice*, Barry Schwartz explains, "The disappointment will be especially severe when the goods we are consuming are 'durable' goods such as cars, houses, stereo systems, elegant clothes, jewelry, and computers. When the brief period of real enthusiasm wanes, people still have these things around them—as a constant reminder that consumption isn't all it's cracked up to be, that expectations are not matched by reality."

People Who Focus on Buying for the Good Life Are Less Happy

It doesn't seem logical that the more things you have, the less satisfied you will be. But researchers have found that to be true. Some of it has to do with why you felt you needed so much in the first place. If you're on what has been called the "hedonic treadmill," very little that you acquire will please you for long, and you will need to buy new and better stuff to recapture your initial sense of satisfaction. What was meant to impress other people either has or has not done its job.

Social economists Richard Ryan and Tim Kasser spent ten years studying the life satisfaction of people who were materialistically oriented versus those to whom other pursuits were more important. In *The High Price of Materialism*, Dr. Kasser notes, "People who strongly value the pursuit of wealth and possessions report lower psychological well-being. . . . They also experienced more physical symptoms and less in the way of positive emotions. Something about a strong desire for materialistic pursuits actually affected the participants' day-to-day lives and decreased the quality of their daily experience."

Part of the reason is that you may feel you're being judged for what you have or don't have, and if your standards are based on what you see in magazines or on television, you will never measure up.

Think back to when you and your friends were newly out of school and living in small apartments, starter homes, or military housing. When you visited each other, you all squeezed in, talked candidly, and had a wonderful time. There was little thought of impressing each other with what you had. But gradually you may have developed a lifestyle in which your status became tied up in the image you presented. If so, it's time to get back to the essential you.

Understand What You Are Buying

With this type of accumulation, we have to realize why we bought the things in the first place before we let them go. Otherwise, we will just go out and replace them with something similar. In fact, the idea of scaling back your stuff may seem in a way like undoing everything you've done up to now to arrive where you are. The fear is that if you let go of even one aspiration or yardstick, everything will fall apart.

But you don't have to turn into an ascetic, especially if you are satisfied with what you currently have. You just have to look closely at all the other former items that you still may be holding on to. And in the future you have to ask yourself what the item you want to buy means to you. If it is an expensive pair of shoes, what do you expect them to do for you? If it is a golf club endorsed by Tiger Woods, what is the significance of that? Ask yourself if you are buying "up" simply because it's what's expected of you when you already have something similar. In other words, figure out the promises implicit in whatever the item is and whether they can come true.

DANGEROUS PHRASES

- "At this age, I should have _____."
- "Someone in my position needs _____."
- "The kids feel left out when they don't have the newest one."
- "These shoes are so last season."
- "Everyone I know already has a _____."
- "There's nothing wrong with it, except it's last year's."
- "They mustn't be doing that well."
- "My things show people who I am."

STUFF LIST #6

Think about items you still have that have been replaced by others more up-to-date or with more status or about things you bought that have not lived up to their implicit promise. Don't forget the items you bought because you felt you were expected to have them in your position but which you are not really using. Then list them here or in your notebook. For disposition, you have a choice of keep, toss, recycle, give away, or sell.

Item	Why I'm Keeping It	Disposition

_____ _____ _____

_____ _____ _____

   Before you buy anything that promises more than the actual item
in the future, you can ask yourself:

_____

_____

Exercise

Once you have filled in the "Disposition" column, use the dot system (described at the end of Chapter 2) to identify everything that's
on its way out.

7

"I Paid Good Money for This!"

Many years ago I attended an estate auction on Long Island. Although I was barely close enough to see what was being offered, my interest was caught by a set of delicate wine glasses with an intricate design. Bidding was for one of them with the understanding that if you won, you would take the other eleven at the same price.

The bidding seemed reasonable—$3.50, then $4.00, and up—and after a while I was the winner. It wasn't until I multiplied my bid by twelve that I realized I now owned some expensive wine glasses.

But it was a beautiful set, and I used them for holidays and special occasions. It was a beautiful set, that is, except the glasses were so dainty that they only held one swallow. Guests had to keep asking for more wine until it seemed as if we were entertaining a group of fallen AAers.

Every time this awkwardness occurred, I felt annoyed with the situation. But the glasses were so pretty and they had been so expensive that we seemed joined for life. Yet I knew what I had to do. One hot July day I bundled them up and brought them to a charity thrift shop. I've never been sorry.

But what if I had paid $100 each for them? My guess is that they would still be sitting on a shelf in my cabinet. Probably I would have found another use for them, if only to hold holiday-colored M&Ms.

Here's another example. You pay $9.95 for a pair of casual summer sandals on sale. They are a half-size smaller than you usually wear, but they feel OK in the shop and you figure they'll stretch a little. But when you try to wear them, they squeeze your toes badly; you don't put them on again for the rest of the summer. In September, rather than take the trouble to store them, you give the shoes away.

You pay $250 for a pair of dress sandals with more of a pedigree. They seem a little narrow in the shop but feel fine, and everything else about them is perfect. The first time you wear them, the straps chafe the sides of your feet. The second time, by the end of the evening, you are in agony. The soles of the shoes are scuffed, so you can't return them to the store, but you don't give them away either. They go back in your closet. Periodically, you will try to wear them to see if anything has changed. It hasn't. But it will be several years before you are able to let them go.

Payment Depreciation

We can quickly get rid of something we paid little for but feel we have to hold on to an expensive item for a longer time. Richard H. Thaler, in his article "Mental Accounting Matters," explains that, in the case of the expensive purchase, we can't get rid of it until what we paid has been fully recouped or "depreciated." Even if we are not using whatever it is, we feel that we have to hold on to it until we have psychologically gotten our money's worth. The fact that we have kept something for a certain length of time seems to allay its cost.

When Virginia pulls a coat out of her closet and says, "I can't give this away yet, I've only worn it twice," she's not saying that she expects to wear the coat until it is threadbare. She's saying that it has not had a chance to depreciate and that she'll probably have to wear it a few more times before it does. Once a piece of clothing is out of style and thus not valuable to *anyone*, it can be considered paid for.

In the case of an object that does not go out of fashion, such as an expensive scroll saw or sterling silver pen, we may attach a fantasy to it. We imagine that we'll someday use it to build a replica of the beautiful table we saw in Williamsburg or write the opening lines of a great novel. No matter that the pen scratches every time we try to write with it and we can't figure out the directions for the saw. Once we learn to use it right, its magical powers will be ours.

Opportunity Costs

Another economic principle, hand in glove with depreciation, is that of opportunity cost. Suppose you have set aside a certain amount to spend on sprucing up your living room. You, and any other family members involved, are torn between an artistic, expensive lamp versus a more ordinary lamp and a leather footstool. After some discussion, you go for the pricey fixture. The lamp looks wonderful, especially when you remind yourself of how much it cost, but the real problem is that it seems to go through lightbulbs at a terrifying rate. When you finally call the store, they acknowledge that it is Italian-made and may be a little high-powered. But it is past the thirty-day return limit, and anyway you no longer have the packaging.

So you grit your teeth and feel annoyed every time it goes dark, but you hang on to the lamp. Because you opted to buy it instead of the other lamp and footstool, you feel a certain amount of regret when you look at the place where the footstool would have gone and imagine yourself lounging comfortably with your feet up. But if you give away the expensive lamp now, you will be forgoing not only it but the other lamp and footstool you could have bought as well.

Life is full of choices, and the specter of what we didn't buy or do is always there. This is the opportunity cost. If we are happy with our purchase and use it, we don't think much about what we passed up. But if we consider getting rid of our selection prematurely, the unchosen alternative often rears its head and adds to our reason for holding on.

Return of the Endowment Effect

We already talked about the endowment effect (see Chapter 2), the emotional reaction that can make removing *anything* from your life feel like a loss. In the case of something expensive, we had certain expectations when we purchased it—that it would significantly improve our day-to-day living or create more fun or romance in our lives or make us seem intelligent or discerning. So we are losing those hopes along with the object itself.

Ralph, a fifty-something friend, bought an expensive graphite tennis racquet. He started private lessons and had fantasies of striding onto the court, lithe and attractive, and delivering killer serves. But after a month he twisted his knee reaching for a low return, adding to a problem he had already started experiencing while playing. When he went to a sports doctor, he was told that unless he had a knee operation, he would not be serving aces anytime soon. Since his knee wasn't troubling him otherwise, he chose to forgo the operation and considered himself lucky. But he still felt some sadness when he passed the racquet along to his nephew.

"But I've Put Too Much into It!"

This is especially true if you "paid good money" for something that either needed physical work or demanded an additional financial outlay. Or perhaps you paid little for it, such as a sailboat our neighbors got at a great price, only to find out that fixing it

Household Endangered Species #7
An expensive espresso machine that came highly recommended but which you can't figure out how to use without flooding the kitchen. Unfortunately, the directions are in Italian.

up would be a major expense. The first summer they couldn't use it at all because it needed extensive scraping and refinishing. Then they had to get new sails and an auxiliary motor. Everyone advised them to sell the boat before they had to pay even more to store it during the winter.

But Rob was adamant. "I've put so much *agitata* into it, I'm not giving up without even sailing it!"

The following summer they took the boat out several times. But their children were bored with a whole day on the water, and Rob's wife, Carol, became seasick. They soon decided that sailing was not for them. Fortunately, they were able to make a better decision—as I'll explain.

"What Was I Thinking?"

Sometimes expensive items are impulse buys, especially when they can't be returned, such as artwork or an auction or tag sale find. We may start to doubt the wisdom of our purchase as soon as we get it home. Added to buyer's remorse is the thought that we have wasted good money. So we try to put up with whatever it is and convince ourselves that it was a good idea after all. And if it was a good idea, there's no reason to give it away prematurely.

I sometimes ask my audiences how they feel when they see that unused juicer or exercise equipment, those expensive craft materials still in the bag, the foreign language tapes that they were too busy to listen to before their trip, the expensive shoes that hurt their feet, the antique clock that can't be repaired. They say that the items make them feel guilty.

I tell them there's enough in life to feel guilty about without adding something unnecessary. In the case of an item that seemed like a good idea at the time, I suggest that they give it a second chance. That is, set a date by which they will start using or displaying it. If they are able to, they have added another dimension to their lives. If they can't, rather than continue to feel guilty, they need to get it out of their sight—and I don't mean by putting it in the basement. They need to find another home for it where it will be appreciated.

Attitude Shifts

In order to ease your guilt, consider the following counterbalancing ideas.

A Mistake Isn't the End of the World

People sometimes make terrible mistakes in life, grave errors in judgment: they embezzle money, race away from a hit-and-run accident, cheat insurance companies, ruin a friend's reputation. They do things that, if not against the law, are trespasses against the moral code most of us live by. And what have you done? Bought a rowing machine you don't use anymore. It was paid for with your own money; chances are no one in your family went hungry because of your purchase.

Or you may have bought clothing that did not quite suit you because you were facing a deadline and needed something to wear or you were having a bad day and it made you feel better. The fact that you are no longer using an item may signal no more than that you've changed and matured, that your interests have moved on. But even if it was an impulse purchase, it was not a crime. It would be nice if we were 100 percent efficient in everything we did, eating only what was good for us, purchasing only what we would use, never wasting time playing computer solitaire. But it's more interesting to be human.

We learn and grow from our mistakes as much as from our successes. I once read a magazine article showing a balcony patio created by an interior designer. It seemed inspired, the kind of breathtaking spot you would never want to leave. In the story, he mentioned dryly that his family and friends had benefited greatly from receiving all the things he had bought and tried that he thought would work in the space but didn't.

If it can happen to professionals, why beat yourself up?

Payment Depreciation Is Natural but Not Rational

What sense does it make to let a pair of shoes stay in the closet unworn for years, to let a silver tea set sit on the sideboard until it tarnishes, or to keep an unused *Encyclopædia Britannica* set until it is outdated? You are not using it; if anything, it is creating negative energy. The more rational idea is that once you realize you cannot use something, you should sell it or give it to someone who can before its time runs out. If you're concerned about the moral high road, wasting something that could be used by someone else only compounds the error.

Learn from the Experience

It's helpful to think about the reasons why you bought something that fell short of your expectations. Maybe you were at an auction (real or online) and you got swept up in the competition. Perhaps you were on vacation and your purchase seemed imbued with the mystique of where you were; you were sure that having it would make your vacation last longer. You may have been shopping with a friend or spouse who pushed you to buy something you weren't sure about.

In her entertaining book *Cleaning and the Meaning of Life*, Paula Jhung talks about what your urges might be telling you. "Does that black leather jacket mean you're finally ready for that Harley? Does a craving for silk tap pants and a lace bustier tell you it's time to take a lover?"

Expand that thought from clothing to almost anything. Perhaps what you bought—or were tempted to buy—only meant you did not follow the trail far enough. What you thought was a shortcut to fill-ing a need was only the first step. If you bring home a set of pastels and a sketch pad, only to find you don't really know how to use them, it may mean that you need to get involved in art classes. If you buy something on impulse, see where it wants to take you.

My neighbors Rob and Carol were able to see that while sailing was not for them, the water still had great appeal. They sold their renovated sailboat and bought a fiberglass motor craft, which they could take out for quick, exciting rides. They plan to use it for water-skiing when the kids get a little older.

It was a circuitous path, but life can take strange twists. So ask yourself what your "mistake" may be telling you.

Make a Profit

Sometimes you have used something but come to the point where it no longer serves your needs. You might still be thinking, "But I paid good money for this! It's too good to just let go." What you're saying is that losing money by giving it away or passing it on seems unacceptable. If you feel that way and it is something with resale value, you have the option of putting an ad in the paper, taking it to an antique dealer or an eBay store, or selling it online yourself. There's more information about selling in Chapter 22, where I talk about options for disposal.

Realize That Your Well-Being Trumps Other Considerations

As I've said before, the bottom-line question is, "How will this make my life better?" Keeping something that doesn't work well or that you don't use creates dead energy. It gets in the way and brings up negative feelings whenever you see it. To offset the strong pull of payment depreciation, you need to ask yourself a second question: "If this thing were destroyed by a fire or a flood, would I replace it?" If the answer is no, then you know what you have to do.

DANGEROUS PHRASES

- ■ "I paid good money for this!"
- ■ "I'll get to it when I have more time."
- ■ "It's too good to just give away!"
- ■ "It would cost me a lot more if I ever had to replace it."
- ■ "If I don't like it, I can always return it."
- ■ "I've put too much into it already to abandon it now."
- ■ "Maybe my feet will shrink."

STUFF LIST #7

It's time to identify the shoes, decorative mistakes, unused woodworking or kitchen utensils—anything for which the price is a consideration in deciding whether to keep it. Look around your home and in your closets, then list the items here or in your notebook. For disposition, you have a choice of keep, toss, recycle, give away, or sell. Use the dot system (described in Chapter 2) to indicate where items are going.

Item	Why I'm Keeping It	Disposition

_____ _____ _____

_____ _____ _____

When you are tempted in the future to hold on to something just because of what it cost, you can tell yourself:

_____

_____

8

Stocking the Bunker

"I'll bet this is the worst mess you've ever seen!" people sometimes joke nervously when they let me in the door.

"Not at all," I'll tell them. "I've been in places where there was so much stuff I couldn't even find the kitchen."

In that particular situation we ate lunch on folding chairs in the driveway and exchanged high fives when we cleared a path to the stove. Suzanne didn't *want* to live that way, but she felt powerless to control her hoarding, and it had gotten worse and worse. People seeing Suzanne, an attractive and well-dressed young professional, in her office would never have believed her living situation.

But true hoarding is a difficult condition to treat. Scientific studies have shown that compulsive hoarders have different patterns of brain activity and less activity in the areas that handle things such as choosing between conflicting options. Many of the hoarders I have encountered are already in therapy and on medication for depression or obsessive-compulsive disorder. If they aren't and they want to change their lives, I'll often suggest psychiatric help.

So why am I even attempting to discuss the condition here? For two reasons. You may be a hoarder who is finally desperate enough to face your fears and start making changes. Just as important, you may not be a true hoarder. You may simply have been overwhelmed by an emotional trauma or are stockpiling things from a need to be prepared for any future emergencies. In milder cases, it is possible to change your thinking and adapt alternatives on your own. And think of it this way: any changes you are able to make will be helpful.

For hoarders who need step-by-step guidance, a good place to start is with the book *Overcoming Compulsive Hoarding* by Fugen Neziroglu, Jerome Bubrick, and Jose A. Yaryura-Tobias. The authors, a psychiatrist and two psychologists from the Bio-Behavioral Institute in Great Neck, New York, specialize in obsessive-compulsive disorder and are experienced in treating hoarding. The book will walk you · through very specific processes and cognitive exercises.

If you feel that no one could be as bad as you are, take a look at the website squalorsurvivors.com. On the site various former hoarders tell their stories and post amazing before-and-after photos of the rooms of their homes.

Making Distinctions

For a true hoarder, the underlying motive is fear. Fear that you will want something or need to know some information in the future and not have it. Fear that you will let something "unique" go and never be able to find it again. Fear that you will accidentally throw away something important or that someone else in your family will. Fear of putting something out of sight so that you won't be able to locate it.

While it's dangerous to generalize, the people I have known with the most extreme stockpiling problems have had a traumatic loss in their lives. Many either lost a parent at a young age or had a child who died. In some cases, they seemed to be holding on to stuff and accumulating more as an effort either to buttress themselves against future tragedy or to fill a perceived void. It got so that when I entered a household that was out of control, I would look for the underlying loss in order to better help them—and I always found it.

These were not events that had happened recently. In the case of a fresh loss, it is natural to let things slide for a while or hold on to the deceased's belongings or feel it is disloyal to move on into a new life. In the situations I saw, the trauma had usually occurred years earlier—but it was having an ongoing effect.

Worst-Case Scenarios

In Chapter 2 I talked about overpersonalizing objects to the extent that we feel we have to protect them. In Chapter 4 I discussed the hold that information can have over us to the point that we feel we need to read *everything*. These are both areas that hoarders have difficulty with. Other areas include anxiety when attempting to discard anything and the fear of not having something when it is needed in the future.

How else can you tell whether you are a hoarder? Here are some characteristics:

- You can no longer sleep in your bed because it is covered with clothes, magazines, boxes, or other items.
- Your plumbing leaks, but you can't have it fixed because you are ashamed to let a repairman in the house.
- You refuse to leave the house because you have to protect your stuff from thieves and family members.
- You have credit card debt from compulsive buying.
- Your spouse cannot tolerate your hoarding any longer and is threatening to move out.
- Your children are upset because it's embarrassing to bring friends home.
- Your neighbors call the fire marshal, and you are given a court order to get rid of nearly everything.

Sad to say, these things actually happen. A Michigan woman who was ordered to clean up her house had an estimated twenty tons of stuff. That's forty thousand pounds. Picture everything from soda cans, Styrofoam cups, and TV dinner trays to broken chairs, bicycles, and seven computer monitors she had picked up on trash pickup day.

"My intention was to find homes for them," she said wistfully. This middle-aged woman is a college graduate and has some insight into her problem. She just can't resist anything.

Fixer-Uppers

Finding good homes and helping other people at the same time was a major concern for the woman from Michigan. On trash pickup day, she took home a bicycle that she planned to fix up and give to the son of a friend. But, as reporter Christine Rook noted in the *Lansing State Journal*, "Perfectionism, procrastination and indecision, though, conspired. The bike remained where she left it [resting against an old suitcase in the living room]."

These kinds of good intentions can sink anyone. If you have a hard time getting things done for yourself, such as mending a screen door properly or taking a jacket to be tailored or a small appliance to be repaired, undertaking renovation work for someone else is only a pipe dream. In the case of the bike, the issue probably wasn't just getting it fixed up; it was making it look like new or at least appealing enough for a child to want to ride. Not being a mechanic would make it even harder, and if the tires were shot, it could mean an outlay of money. Sometimes by the time you finish fixing something up, it will have cost you more than just buying one in working order.

Curb Appeal

It's a temptation for hoarders when they see something discarded by the curb to feel they have to rescue it, but we can all fall into the trap of thinking someone could use an item—either someone we know or an unknown person in need. I think that putting items by the curb is a fine idea; I have done it and been gratified to see them disappear.

But if you are already cluttered, bringing in more could swamp the boat. And if it is something you bring home to fix up for someone else, it can easily swamp you.

Bulking Up

Warehouses that sell only large amounts—for example, gallon jars of mayonnaise and a dozen rolls of paper towels—and offer them at a discount are a recent phenomenon. It makes sense to shop at one of these places if you have a business or large family—and have outbuildings to store supplies in. But bulk is bulk. To fill up a pantry with extras to the point where you can barely walk inside to find what you need, or a basement that could be used for something more exciting than stockpiling toilet paper, is not worth the money saved or the guarantee that you will never run out. The great majority of us don't live miles from the nearest town or convenience store; running out of an item is not a catastrophe, especially when you compare it with the way overstuffing your space will be.

Attitude Shifts

To stop yourself from practicing overstocking behaviors, review the following counterbalancing ideas.

Household Endangered Species #8
The dresser you bought at an antique auction some years ago, intending to remove the seven coats of black lacquer and repair the drawers. You tried, once.

Recognize the Seriousness of Your Problem

Suzanne came from a family of savers and had never liked throwing anything away. But she had always been in a situation, either in a college dorm or when living with roommates and then

THE WORST THAT CAN HAPPEN

Compared with some of the more dire consequences of hoarding, letting things go is mild by comparison. Get in the habit of asking yourself, "What is the worst thing that can happen if I . . ."

- "run out of paper towels or shampoo or pens"
- "bundle up most of my plastic and paper bags and return them to the store recycling bin"
- "throw out an envelope of coupons that came in the mail without opening it"
- "recycle a charity's or organization's newsletter without stopping to read it"
- "say, 'No, thanks,' to a friend who's getting rid of her old La-Z-Boy recliner"
- "can't find the birthday card I bought to send to _____ _____"
- "learn my partner has discarded the stack of yellowing newspapers in the shed"

At worst you may feel anxious, worry about lost opportunities, and wonder whether those plastic bags will be properly recycled. You will be temporarily inconvenienced and have to go to the store to buy more supplies or another card. But those feelings will pass. And it will get easier.

a boyfriend, where she had to keep her hoarding under control. When she and her fiancé split up unexpectedly, however, she relocated to a small cottage and moved into "rescue" mode. Everything deserved to be saved, even the circulars that came in the mail. By the time we met, she knew she had crossed the line into hoarding.

"I have to treat it like an addiction," she said frankly. "That's what it is! There are situations I just can't put myself in, situations that are toxic for me. I have a post office box now and don't even look at what I'm discarding. I just bring home bills and personal letters."

So far Suzanne is winning the battle. First she started seeing a therapist and was put on an antidepressant, then she began to identify the behaviors at her vulnerable points. She's started dating again, thanks to Match.com, and seems to be on her way to a fulfilling life.

The More You Do Something, the Easier It Gets

The first few times you introduce new thoughts and behaviors can feel awkward and leave you plagued with doubts. The first time you skip buying an industrial-sized package; the first time you drive past a tag sale or curbside discard without stopping; the first time you tell a friend, "No, thanks," when she offers you her old color TV and you don't even worry about finding someone who could use it; the first time you discard a jar with the remains of a candle inside that you're sure you could clean out and use for something.

These things will all be difficult at first and may cause you anxiety. But when you keep doing them, they will become habits and feel easier and easier. You will also have the reinforcement of more space and the promise of a cleared-out home. Even if you don't see it in the beginning, everything you do is an improvement.

Curbside Finds Have a Price Tag

Unless you have a definite use for a discarded item and can put it where it belongs as soon as you get it home, whatever you pick up is going to cost you. It is going to take up space you don't have and may need repairing; at best, it is one more thing to be responsible for until you can bring yourself to say good-bye. Suppose you are driving along and see a microwave oven waiting by the curb for garbage pickup. You don't know if it works, but you are sure you know people who can use one. Alas, when you get the microwave home and try it out, it doesn't work, after all. But now it's yours. So you stack it with all your other rescues that are waiting to be repaired.

If you have trouble resisting curbside finds, stay home on days when items are discarded, or take another route to work. Remind yourself that most of the stuff waiting for trash pickup is there for a reason. Also remind yourself that it's very hard to choose something for someone else and that you can end up storing items for a long time. You don't want it to be until the Public Health Department arrives.

You Can *Say No to "Gifts"*

When someone offers us a discard, there is always the slightest possibility that we can use it for something. Furthermore, people are happy when we say yes; it solves their disposal problem and lets them feel that whatever it is will be going to a good home. It makes them feel happy that they can do a favor for someone else. The more you get a reputation for accepting anything, the more things people will offer to you, from sofas to stray cats.

But, like curbside finds, these things are not free either. When something is given to you by a friend or relative, a sense of obligation is created. You are expected to be grateful, perhaps reciprocate in kind, or at least show that you are getting good use from the item. Your hands are tied if you decide you cannot use it after all.

What do you feel when you say, "No, thank you"? It may seem as if you are rejecting the donor and that person's offering is not good enough for you. You may be afraid that you are closing the door on an important opportunity. Taking the item may feel like a chance to solidify your relationship. Or you may be worried that it will end up in a landfill if you don't give it a home. It may be a combination of all those things.

But look what you get when you say no. One less thing to store, take care of, worry about, and find a use for. If the item needs work, it means you won't be taking on a further obligation for which you don't have time. Remember that such a donation is rarely an exact fit, something you would have gone out and bought yourself; you have to stretch to accommodate it. If you say no often enough, people will stop offering you anything and everything. Rather than face rejection, they'll wait until it's something really worthwhile, something you desperately need. And then, you may say yes.

DANGEROUS PHRASES

- "I'll keep it just in case."
- "You never know when you might run out."
- "It's fun to feel surprised when you find something you'd forgotten about!"
- "I'll just put it here for now."
- "I'll do it tomorrow when I'm not so depressed."
- "I've *always* been like this."
- "It just needs some TLC and it'll work fine."
- "I don't know why I even bother trying to clean up."
- "Better to be safe than sorry."
- "I know someone who could use that!"
- "Buying a lot at one time means not having to shop so often."

STUFF LIST #8

Although you may feel that you save everything, there are categories that are more of a temptation for you than others. Look around and identify those as well as things that you rescued but that are not being used. Ask yourself these questions:

- "How does this make my life better?"
- "What is the worst thing that can happen if I get rid of it?"

Then list these things here or in your notebook. For disposition, you have a choice of keep, toss, recycle, give away, or sell. Use the dot system (described in Chapter 2) to indicate where items are going. Trash everything portable immediately.

Item	Why I'm Keeping It	Disposition

_____   _____   _____

_____   _____   _____

_____   _____   _____

_____   _____   _____

_____   _____   _____

When you are tempted to rescue an item, accept something free, or buy more than you need in the future, you can tell yourself:

_____

_____

9

"I Want It Now!"

When I arrived to help Bob and Marsha move from a house to a condo, I was struck by the number of videos they had on shelves and the stacks and stacks of mass market paperbacks on every surface. These would be an easy discard.

Wrong.

"You're going to keep all of them?" I asked finally.

"Why not?"

I focused on the tapes. "Do you really think you'll watch them all again? With new DVDs coming out all the time?"

"Probably not," said Bob, a compact, ruddy-faced man with a cockatoo crest of white hair. By contrast, Marsha was a delicate gray dove. "But if we decide we want to see something, it's right here."

"You could get it from the library or video store. Or through Netflix."

They looked unhappy. "But then we'd have to *wait*," Marsha said.

"Besides," Bob chimed in, "we already have these. What's the point of giving them away?"

I had an answer to that, but for the time being, we moved on to another room.

Why Wait?

Why do we have such a horror of waiting for anything? In part, we have gotten out of practice. The pace of our world has picked up to the point of needing everything immediately, often as soon as it comes to mind. We can get so many movies "on demand" that we never have to leave the den. Supermarkets and convenience stores are often open all night.

Everything seems to reinforce our feelings of, "I don't want to wait, I shouldn't have to wait, I want it *now*." But there is also another dynamic at work here—the idea of infinite choice. "I might want to reread *Moby Dick*, play Monopoly, dress in bright green for St. Patrick's Day. I might want to watch those "Seinfeld" tapes again, go back to lifting weights again, learn to ice sculpt."

"Don't Fence Me In"

Living in the land of freedom, we believe we are entitled to infinite choice. And it often seems as if that is what we have. When we open our closets in the morning, many people can select from enough shirts, slacks, dresses, or shoes to stock a small boutique. As one attractive woman in a workshop told me, "When I need something new, I've learned to 'shop' my closet. Usually I can find what I'm looking for."

But a serious problem arises when the salesperson of complete freedom meets the greedy child of instant gratification; then it becomes necessary to have everything we might want within easy reach. Think about that for a minute, then multiply it by books, shoes, tools, purses, vid-

Household Endangered Species #9
A collection of temporarily single socks. You know that as soon as you discard them, their mates will show up. If not, you can always make them into sock monkeys.

eos, spices, craft materials, DVDs, specialty clothing, sports gear, and so on. It's dizzying.

These concepts are simple to grasp, and I won't belabor the point. If the phrases "I *might* want to . . ." and "I need it now!" are part of your everyday vocabulary, then you may be cluttered with your options. Fortunately, there are a number of counterbalancing ideas that can help you make changes.

Attitude Shifts
Consider the following counterbalancing ideas.

Familiarity Breeds Neglect
Life is always coming at us with something new: a review of a wonderful book or movie, a recommendation for a play from a friend, something fascinating in the mail, word-of-mouth information from everywhere. We live in a swirl of choices. These options seem compelling and make us anxious to keep up with what is going on. New things hold the promise of novelty, of new answers to life's questions.

So where does that leave everything we already own and may or may not have read or watched or used? From what I can see, exactly where it has been since we placed it there originally. As a law of physics decrees, "Bodies at rest tend to remain at rest." The longer we own something, the less exciting it seems. We either already know or suspect we know the information it has to offer us.

A simple example is what happened when VCRs first came out. Suddenly people could tape TV shows and movies to watch at another time. As soon as they could figure out how to set up their VCRs, they started taping. They taped programs whenever they went out and also when they were home but watching something more compelling. They taped the shows they were watching so they would be able to see them again whenever they wanted. But there were new shows to constantly watch and tape. After a while, last month's sitcom faded in importance until it was just taking up space on the shelf.

I pointed out to Bob and Marsha that new movies almost always seemed more exciting than ones they were already familiar with. When I asked how many of their videotapes they had watched again in the past year, Marsha remembered seeing *It's a Wonderful Life* at Christmas. But that was the only one.

"You could pick out your favorites and give the rest to the veterans' home," I suggested.

And that is what they did. It was funny to hear their comments as they went through their tapes, finding many they had forgotten or never knew they had. *"Pretty in Pink?"* Bob said, incredulous. "That one must be yours, Marsh."

"No, Susan borrowed it from someone and left it here. I can't believe you taped a whole season of Mets games. These won't be making the cut!"

By the time they had finished, they were gloating. "We can keep these in the cabinet under the TV and get rid of the bookcase the others were in," Bob said. "I never liked that bookcase anyhow."

A Change of Taste

Along with our society, Bob and Marsha and the rest of us are constantly evolving. If you are involved in music, literature, film, fashion, cuisine, wine, woodworking, and so on, you already know how your tastes keep developing. The more we learn, the faster we move beyond what we once enjoyed. According to Barry Schwartz in *The Paradox of Choice*, "As we have contact with items of high quality, we begin to suffer from 'the curse of discernment.' The lower quality items that used to be perfectly acceptable are no longer good enough." Yet even when we sense that fact, we tend to hang on out of habit.

Anticipation Creates Savor

One of the things that makes us look back on childhood with so much nostalgia is that we didn't get everything we wanted as soon as we wanted it. We dreamed of certain items, begged for them, and sometimes they arrived for Christmas, Hanukkah, or our birthday. Often we spent more time enjoying the anticipation of the gift than we received pleasure from it once it was ours.

Anticipation gives life saliency. Our initial response is to want what we want immediately. But when we become reconciled to having to wait, either because we have ordered something that's out of stock or are getting it as a gift, our pleasure at receiving it is much greater than if we walked over and plucked it off the shelf. Once we deal with the slight dip in mood when we realize we won't have it on demand, our pleasure is greater when it does arrive.

Important Things Become Part of You

"If I don't have it on the shelf where I can see it, I'll forget it was my favorite movie."

Hmm. You saw it, you loved it, it evidently became part of you. What is so terrible about not having it constantly at the top of your mind? What does it matter if you can't remember the title or who was in it, if you have the warmth of your memory? You have seen wonderful films in the past and anticipate seeing more in the future, and it may not be your favorite for that much longer.

If it's that important to you to remember, make a list and keep it at the front of your file cabinet. For that matter, you can list all the videos and books you're giving away that you really liked. If you have a yen to watch or reread something you can't quite recall, go to your list. Then take the book or DVD out of your library or buy it if you want. But remember that some memories are better left unvisited. You will not be approaching *Look Homeward, Angel* or *Catcher in the Rye* or *Breakfast at Tiffany's* or *E.T.* as the same person who originally loved it.

Hierarchies

An Italian economist, Vilfredo Pareto, discovered that approximately 80 percent of the land in Italy was owned by 20 percent of the population, that 80 percent of the income in Italy belonged to 20 percent of the people, and so on. This principle, adapted by Joseph M. Juran, was found to be applicable to other areas; for example, 20 percent of the sales force produces 80 percent of the company profits. It can work equally well in assessing your clothes or your kitchen utensils.

But people often cite the 20/80 rule as if it's an all-or-nothing principle. It's true that we generally use 20 percent of our belongings 80 percent of the time. We wear the same clothes, use the same group of cosmetics, and so on. But too often the other 80 percent gets lumped in a category of seldom-to-never usage, which ignores the fact that there's a whole gradation, items that we use 25 or 30 percent of the time as opposed to 5 percent. It is not an all-or-nothing proposition.

There's also the matter of how strongly we need something, even if it's not that often. You may wear a down-filled jacket most of the time in the winter and a cloth coat for only a few dressy occasions per year. But for those special occasions, the cloth coat is the coat you want. Though you only infrequently use a thermal holder to keep coffee warm, it can be essential when you're hosting a gathering—but you can get through life quite happily without a melon-ball shaper, ice cube trays in the shapes of playing card symbols, or special gardening clogs.

The point is, when we are talking about having items on demand and are considering what we might want or need, we need to be discriminating about the probabilities of use. Decide whether, in the unlikely event of wanting something you've discarded, you can rent it reasonably or borrow it. Think about whether there will be a future occasion when you will definitely need something, even though you don't use it very frequently. Also ask yourself what else you could use in its place if you didn't have it.

I was helping a friend optimize the space in her apartment and suggested under-the-bed storage for some inactive files she needed to keep. It turned out that the space wasn't available; for the past seven years, she had had her parents' aluminum folding table, still in its dusty carton, under there.

"Want me to help you move it out?"

"I don't know," she said slowly. "I might use it sometime."

"What?" I teased. "If you suddenly decide to have sixteen people over for Thanksgiving?"

"Yes! That's what my parents used it for, for when we had company."

It was such an unlikely scenario for her that we both laughed. I pointed out that if she didn't have the table, she could just rent one; she would need to rent chairs anyway.

She's thinking about it.

DANGEROUS PHRASES

- "I *might* want to _____."
- "I can't give it away because I promised to lend it to someone. I just need to remember who."
- "If I don't see it, I'll forget how much I like it."
- "If I get it from the library, I'll have to remember to take it back."
- "A bird in the hand is worth two in the bush."
- "Borrowing things makes me feel obligated."
- "I need it *now*."

STUFF LIST #9

Think about those things you're saving because you *might* want to watch or otherwise use them sometime, the things you bought impulsively because you wanted them immediately but which didn't quite live up to your expectations. Then list them here or in your notebook. For disposition, you have a choice of keep, toss, give away, or sell.

Item	Why I'm Keeping It	Disposition

_____   _____   _____

_____   _____   _____

When in the future you feel like you have to have something immediately and must therefore buy it rather than borrow or rent it, you
can tell yourself:

_____

_____

Exercise

If you have a number of items, such as assorted videos or CDs, you
may use the dot system (described in Chapter 2) to indicate where
items are going.

10

"It's Part of My Collection!"

One afternoon when I was about six, we had an important visitor. I don't remember what made Mrs. Archibald so distinguished, but my mother and grandmother hurriedly set out pastel wafers, Jordan almonds, nonpareils, and thin mints, as if they were opening a candy store.

Mrs. Archibald asked me about school. Then she added, "And what do you collect?"

I looked at her blankly.

"Some little girls collect Storybook dolls," she prodded. And then she added firmly, "My grandson collects foreign postage stamps. Every child needs a good hobby."

After that I tried to get one. But I could never understand why I needed more than one of the same thing.

It took me almost twenty years before I finally got it. And then there was no stopping me.

Having been on both sides of the collecting experience, I understand its seductiveness. You buy or are given something interesting. Then somehow you get a second. Once you have two of them, a need to corner the market is born.

What isn't always considered when we discuss this subject is that other people love the idea of your collections, because it makes it easier to buy you gifts. If they think you love penguins or Hummels or antique tools or autographed baseballs, they have one less thing to worry about when your birthday or the holidays roll around. I used to imagine that when people were shopping and came across something with a feline theme, a neon sign screaming "J-U-D-I" began blinking on and off—and I didn't even collect cats; I just lived with two. On the other hand, it took me longer than it should have to realize that my brother had enough frog memorabilia, my son had outgrown funny T-shirts, and my sister-in-law was very discriminating when it came to antique cows.

In the interest of keeping the world clutter free, it's a good idea to check with the people you buy presents for and see if they are still interested in certain categories.

But back to your own collections.

The Joys of Collecting

As Mrs. Archibald said, "Every child needs a good hobby." What she was talking about was the pleasure and concentration of the search, learning how to identify and organize items, and keeping out of trouble. For adults, collecting includes having a purpose for shopping or traveling, camaraderie with other collectors, the thrill of the chase, and pride in showing other people what you have put together.

So if collecting makes everybody happy, why is it a chapter in this book?

It's here because most collections are physical, made up of stuff. And we all know how quickly stuff can get out of hand. Some collected items are small, of course, and fit in a drawer. Others are larger and take up an étagère. Or a garage. But because collections are made up of things that are unique or beautiful but not generally useful, it is important to decide how many collections you want and what you will do with them.

What happens when good collections go bad?

They Go Past Their Shelf Life

People change; interests change. Without getting into the debate of whether life is more satisfying when glimpsed through a single window, the fact is that most people no longer cultivate one life-long interest or even have one lifelong career. That means that what thrilled you ten or twenty years ago has probably lost some luster. Admitting this doesn't mean that your collection was a mistake; it signals that you have satisfied a particular curiosity or need and are ready to move on.

At one time in my life, I loved vintage Coca-Cola trays. They were colorful and attractive, part of our heritage, and the bright-faced young women of the 1940s and 1950s resonated with my childhood. For several years I displayed them in my kitchen—until I no longer really "saw" them. Then I stored the trays away. Finally, I realized that the Coke memorabilia meant much less to me. So I sold the trays on eBay, along with some chocolate molds and many antique cards and valentines, and took a vacation in Key West.

You may counter that even though you are not attached to a collection any longer and not using it in a practical way, it's not *hurting* anything. But that may not be true. One of the principles of feng shui is the importance of keeping the things in your life current. When you don't, there's the danger of being stuck in the past and unable to move ahead in your life. In extreme cases, you won't want to travel or even leave the house because of the threat of break-ins and loss. More likely, if your home is stuffed with your past interests, there isn't room for new items, new experiences, to come in.

In *Clear Your Clutter with Feng Shui*, Karen Kingston points out that by collecting we may be "responding to an intuitive need to gather a particular type of essence that we need for our own personal growth." But this is a process, not a destination. She adds, "Life is constantly changing and moving, and we actually only need to collect that essence for as long as it takes us to integrate it spiritually into our life. Then we can move on to something new."

You know how it feels to be actively engaged in a collection. You read about it, talk to other collectors, hunt for hard-to-find or desirable items, and feel that quickening of spirit when you look at what you have. On the other hand, you know how it feels when the beam is fainter or nonexistent. If that's the case, give yourself every chance to move on.

Collections Try to Take Over Your Life

They don't mean anything by it. You've put a lot of effort into your collection, and it has rewarded you by giving you years of pleasure. It's true that you may have spent money that you will never get back. There has certainly been an investment of time when you might have been doing other things. But how can I suggest that a collection has a tendency to try and take over? Well, consider the story of Ben.

Ben, an accountant in his late thirties, had turned his finished basement into a terminal for his electric trains. He had grown up in an apartment where there was never room for a full layout, although his parents had dutifully given him the HO-gauge sets he craved.

When I first saw the miniature world he had created, I was entranced. Besides buying accessories like railroad crossing gates and tiny people, he had made many beautiful hand-painted buildings. There was plaster snow on the ground; in this old-fashioned scene, it was perpetually a Norman Rockwell winter.

Ben watched my face as I admired the layout and the tiny engines that actually puffed smoke. Then he said sadly, "It's gotten so I hardly come down here. There's nothing left to do. But how can I give it up? I've put years into it!"

"It's wonderful," I agreed and then added, "but is there anything else you'd like to do with the space?"

"What I'd *really* like to do is move to a condo in Miami, right on the beach. I miss water when I can't see it. My folks and my sister are in Florida, and my company is opening an office there. But there wouldn't be room for my trains." He looked at me and laughed. "Is that pathetic? I bet you wouldn't let it keep you from getting on with your life."

I thought about that, imagining that something like the train collection was mine. "Well, I'd want to take lots of photos," I said slowly. "Maybe I'd have someone take a panoramic shot of the whole layout and have that blown up into a mural, which I could put on the wall of my new place. Then I'd contact the town hall and see if they wanted it as a display to put out at holidays. If they didn't, maybe a school or historical society would."

He nodded.

"Even if no organization was interested, I'd contact other collectors for ideas or see if any of them wanted to buy it—you must know hundreds of people! But I'd keep one favorite set that didn't take up a lot of room and display it sometimes."

"Wow. That's what you'd do?"

"I know it wouldn't be easy," I told him truthfully. "But I couldn't let it keep me from the life I really wanted."

"I'll have to think about that!"

I didn't add two other things that had struck me about the beautiful layout: everything was frozen in an eternal winter, and the trains were symbolically going around in circles.

It turned out Ben didn't need to hear that. The trains and layout ended up in the lobby of a children's hospital, protected by a plastic dome and with a small donor plaque, and Ben moved to South Beach. From the postcard he sent me, he was having the time of his life.

Just because you've invested time and energy in your collection doesn't mean that if you move on, it was a waste of time. Your collection filled a need or an interest at the time; having that need or interest satisfied and turning your attention to something else does not negate what it meant to you. Take lots of photos, keep one or two of the best items for your own satisfaction if you want, and find the rest of your collection a good home.

Three Items Don't Make a Collection

For people with strong collecting instincts, owning two or three similar items—by accident or design—awakens the urge for more. All the reasons for collecting come into play: the thrill of the chase, the creation of something new, the pleasure of displaying the items together. It's as seductive as the Sirens' song to hapless sailors. As my friend Stephanie says, "I don't even have to *own* one first. I can get excited just seeing it in a decorating magazine!" As long as I've known her, Stephanie has been attracted by all kinds of Americana. Yet her home does not resemble Ye Olde Cozy Corner.

"What I usually do," she told me, "is go on eBay and see what the things are selling for. That brings me back down to earth."

The truth is, the whole collecting market has changed. Once upon a time, children collected baseball cards and Barbie dolls and Matchbox cars; now adults buy them and keep them in their original packaging. Stumbling across treasures at tag sales or in thrift shops is becoming increasingly rare. "Antiques Roadshow" and online auctions have made even the managers of nonprofit charity shops more savvy when it comes to pricing. Now when you decide to expand two or three items into a full-blown collection, you're making a financial commitment.

But what about items that have no commercial value? It's just as easy to fall into the three-item trap. Here is one scenario. You buy a small plaster alligator with a thermometer in its tummy that catches your eye in a thrift shop. It's not expensive. On the way home you remember that you once had a rubber alligator from a childhood trip to Florida. You've also inherited an alligator-skin purse from your mother. Immediately, you see a shelf of vignettes with other, more interesting reptiles and a tossing of sand and shells. Maybe you'll become known as the foremost collector of alligator memorabilia!

Stop right there. It's only a passing whim. Even if you do collect several other alligator items, it won't amount to anything except some leftover stuff you don't know what to do with.

They don't have to be the start of a collection.

"My Things Are like My Children!"

People have actually said this to me about their collections. It has usually been at one of my presentations, when talking privately afterward. They have confided this about their orchids, sets of china, Lladro figurines, porcelain animals, bisque dolls, and so on. What I believe they mean is that they are happy being among these items, they feel the responsibility of caring for them, and their attachment is fierce. I never argue with them or attempt to change their minds. But if you identify with the idea of your things as children to the extent that you are attached to them and feel responsible for their care, you may want to ask yourself what role they play in your life. Are they a substitute for human relationships or a healthy addition? If you worry about what will happen to them when you're gone, it's important to make appropriate arrangements.

Jill, a widow retired from her job as a UN translator, spoke to me about her collection of porcelain birds and wildlife. It was the kind of work produced in limited editions. She had her collection on display in her home in cabinets and loved looking at it. The downside was that she had no family except for a cousin she rarely saw and who had expressed no interest in the collection. While her friends admired various pieces, none wanted to be responsible for them all.

Suggesting that Jill sell some of the collection was out of the question; she was far too attached and enjoyed it too much for that. I suggested that since the porcelain pieces were made in different series by an established company, there would be clubs and organizations devoted to their acquisition. Such organizations would have websites, and through one of them she might find a young collector

Household Endangered Species #10
A weird condiment that you received as part of a gift basket or hostess gift, which you can't imagine eating but are saving to pass on to someone else.

who would be thrilled to "inherit" her pieces. The benefit was that this would be someone who would keep them together and appreciate their worth.

I had almost forgotten our conversation when Jill sent me an e-mail. "I finally learned how to use my computer!" she wrote. "I've been having the best time comparing notes with other Royal Worcester collectors, and several have invited me to visit them in England! Somehow, being able to enjoy my collection so much now makes me less worried about what will eventually happen to it. Go figure!"

The Collection Really Isn't Yours

"It belonged to my father . . . my grandmother . . . my great-aunt." It's wonderful when you can have one or two meaningful items that were important to a family member and are perfect to remember that person by—but what do you do with a full-blown collection? Having been in this situation myself, I know that inherited collections are a challenge for several reasons. You've seen the love and interest that went into amassing them. You feel they are a part of your heritage. And you may have been told, implicitly or in actual words, that the collection must never be broken up.

Other facts: you have no interest in the collection or the items in it yourself. That is, you don't have the inclination or interest to pore over the various objects and add to them. You don't have the room to display the collection in your home. Perhaps you could use the money that selling it would bring. In any case, keeping it in storage or in cartons in your basement is doing no one any good.

What generally happens in such a situation is that you do nothing for a while. If the collection's owner is recently deceased, you are still processing your loss. Also, you have other physical items to deal with. It could take a year or two before you are ready to consider the complications of the collection. Once you realize that keeping the items indefinitely in storage is not the answer, you'll have some other options to consider.

If you don't need the money it would bring and the collection is significant, you could donate it in its entirety to a museum, historical society, college library, and so on. If it has value but is not museum quality, consider looking for an organization of similar collectors and donating it to their society or to a younger individual who would be ecstatic to have it. Either way, you know it would be treated with respect and the proper reverence.

If that does not interest you, consider doing the following. Take photographs of the items—or at least the most interesting ones—and then divide the collection among your siblings, cousins, children, or other interested parties, keeping for yourself one or two items that particularly represent your relative's interest in the collection. Then sell or donate the rest with a clear conscience. It will be up to each of the recipients to do what they feel is best.

You don't have to feel guilty about whatever steps you take. The original collector undoubtedly relished the process of tracking down and identifying the items and had years of enjoyment showing them to other people. But ultimately the collection consists of only things, of which you have photographs and a good representation. If keeping items that are no longer current in your own life can hold you back, this is even more true for physical things one generation removed. You're responsible for living your own life—that's all.

"I'm Not That Interested in _____ Anymore, but People Won't Stop Giving Them to Me."

This seems to happen more with cute animal memorabilia than with Impressionist paintings or gold coins. I've already talked about how having a collection solves other people's gift-giving dilemmas, so they may not give the practice up without a fight. Obviously, the time to tell friends and relatives you're no longer interested is not right after you've opened another owl mug. Pick a time far away from the holidays or your birthday and point out, "You know, I used to love collecting _____. But now I really have enough. I'll probably be getting rid of some of the ones I have."

But why should you try to head gift givers off at the pass? Why not just thank them and quietly dispose of the item? Because, given the endowment effect, you might have a hard time letting go. It will be hard enough when someone says to you, "I know you said you didn't want any more _____, but this one was too cute to resist"—and you find yourself agreeing with them!

DANGEROUS PHRASES

- "I'm saving my string collection for my grandchildren."
- "So many of these were gifts from dear friends."
- "It's taken me years to find all these rocks!"
- "I hate to abandon something before it's complete."
- "My things are like my children."
- "I could never replace it all if it were stolen."
- "I'll just check what's up for sale on eBay."

STUFF LIST #10

Think about everything you are actively collecting and all your older collections that you don't pay attention to any longer. Think about those bits and pieces of potential collections stored in cabinets or on shelves that never quite got off the ground. You'll be surprised at how many there are. List them here or in your notebook. For disposition, you have a choice of keep, toss, recycle, give away, or sell. If you are reducing collections or have some miscellaneous items that never led anywhere, use the dot system (described at the end of Chapter 2) to indicate where items are going.

Collection	Why I'm Keeping It	Disposition
_____	_____	_____
_____	_____	_____
_____	_____	_____
_____	_____	_____
_____	_____	_____
_____	_____	_____
_____	_____	_____
_____	_____	_____
_____	_____	_____
_____	_____	_____
_____	_____	_____
_____	_____	_____

_____   _____   _____
_____   _____   _____
_____   _____   _____
_____   _____   _____

When you are tempted in the future to hold on to former collections or create a new one because you have three items, you can tell yourself:

_____

_____

11

Knocked for a Loop

For most people, keeping their homes and belongings under control is like swimming in the sea. They can keep afloat and breathe as long as the water stays calm and they aren't distracted. But when a riptide threatens to pull them under or they are menaced by a shark, all order disappears and they come close to drowning. To put it another way, most of us don't have enough wiggle room to keep from going under after a major life change.

Often things fall apart so subtly that we don't connect the two. "I used to be super organized," a new client, Maryanne, tells me, gesturing at her piled-high dining room table. "Now look at this mess. I don't know what happened!"

"You started working at home?" I venture.

"Oh."

Once we had diagnosed the problem, we were quickly able to set up an office system that worked for her. But other upsets are not so easily righted.

When discussing it, people like Maryanne say to me, "I never had a problem before."

"Before what?" I ask.

"Before I had kids."

"Before my mother died and I had her stuff to deal with, too."
"Before I was laid off."
"Before we moved into a bigger house."
"Before I got sick."
"Before I got married again."
"Before we inherited that money."
"Before I started my own business."
"Before I got divorced and had to move to this condo."

And so on. The common denominator is a significant life change, happy or sad, that overturns whatever system had previously been in place. Often that system was not working perfectly, and now it isn't working at all. Perhaps these individuals used to let things pile up all week, and they would straighten them out on Saturday morning. But now there are no more "Saturday mornings." Sometimes they want to think the change is temporary, and they wait for things to get back to "normal" instead of adjusting their lives. But normal never returns, at least not in the same way.

Sometimes you can suffer an emotional downturn without a dramatic cause. When even getting out of bed in the morning takes resolve, your physical world suffers. As a good friend pointed out, "*Everything* goes to hell when I'm depressed!"

How It Happens

When you're busy struggling to find a new direction or to get out from under a traumatic event, stuff creeps in unnoticed. Things get used and are not put back in place. Perhaps you have had to accommodate the belongings of a new spouse or parent or have had to move to a place half the size of your former home. You are working out a schedule to care for a baby or feel traumatized by the breakup of a long-term relationship. At that point your physical environment is the least of your concerns.

Dominique Browning, editor in chief of *House and Garden*, put it well in her book *Around the House and in the Garden*. "When I was divorced my sense of home fell apart. And so, too, did my house. The rooms looked ravaged, sacked as they were of furniture, art, books, the mementos of a life constructed with someone else; everything fallen into disrepair." She goes on to describe years of fits and starts until she regained her equilibrium and her home.

How you handle it—or don't—often has to do with how you feel about the change. If it is something you are happy about, a change you helped to create, it will be easier to adapt and go in a new direction. It feels worthwhile to do whatever is necessary, and you have optimism on your side. But if you are resistant or in denial, your energy is invested in trying to hold on to your former view of yourself.

One of the saddest situations I have ever encountered—at least, at first—was one in which a private agency hired me. I was asked to help a woman about to be evicted from the downstairs half of a split-level home because she was creating a fire hazard.

Lonnie, an anxious, talkative woman, quickly filled me in. First, the "King of the Rats" had divorced her and married his dental assistant. Then, her chronic back pain worsened until she was forced to leave her job as a school secretary and to apply for disability benefits. Eventually, she was forced out of a five-bedroom house and had to move into this downstairs apartment.

The apartment, divided into four rooms, was good sized. But Lonnie had brought all her belongings with her, from lawn furniture to banquet-sized kitchen pots, as well as several semiworking computers. Furthermore, she had no interest in getting rid of anything. On an emotional level, she was sure that what had happened was temporary, a bad dream, and she would be back in her own large house again.

Trying to keep her focused, we worked at getting what we agreed was trash into large plastic bags and recycling cartons. At one point she mentioned that her sister was willing to put a lot of the things into storage in her garage. Feeling sorry for her sister, I nevertheless urged Lonnie to do so. "Oh, I don't know," she said. "Things like that have a way of disappearing."

"But it's better than seeing them put out on the street," I told her. "Besides, you need to do something if you want to stay here."

"I'm not that crazy about this place. I want my own house back!"

Despite Lonnie's feelings of denial, we were able to clear the apartment out sufficiently to keep her from getting evicted. She was not a hoarder but was just someone who was not ready to face a new reality. With her landlord's permission, she and her teenage daughters (who lived with their father) had a giant yard sale and made a considerable profit. Lonnie cheered up further. By then she had realized that with her back problems, four rooms were plenty to care for, and we discussed ways to make her home into a place she loved.

INCONVENIENT TRUTHS

Pretend the following is a true or false quiz:

- Once you have a new baby or two, your home will not be pristine for the foreseeable future.
- If you have a debilitating illness, you will need to simplify the physical care you give your home.
- If you are retired or unemployed, you will not have the structure you had in your former life.
- When you marry or remarry, you will never have complete control over your environment again.
- If you inherit goods from a family member, there will always be more than you need.
- Once your children are grown, with their own homes, keeping their rooms just as they were won't bring those years back.
- When you are bereaved, you will have to deal with that person's belongings before you can create a new life.
- If your income is dramatically reduced, you will need to scale down your lifestyle accordingly.

Most people would agree that the answers to the preceding statements are true, at least most of the time. The truth is, the sooner you are able to admit it when they are true for you, the less drastically your life will fall apart. If they do not apply to you but to someone you know, try cutting the person some slack and offering help when appropriate.

Happy Changes: And Baby Makes Three (or Four)

One of the happiest changes I can think of is welcoming a new baby into your life. It is also one of the most life changing. There will always be another toy to put away, another little shirt to wash, a high chair tray to wipe off—to say nothing of the important things, like cuddling, taking walks, reading books together, and so on. If you have high standards, the best thing you can do is to relax them for a while rather than trying to keep everything up.

What will help is quickly recycling clothes that get too small and toys that are outgrown and simply tossing tattered books, puzzles with missing pieces, and anything else not fit for passing on to someone else. Assess toddlers' artwork and keep the best in a large artist's folder—the rest can go to doting grandparents or into the recycling bag. If you hang on to everything "precious," you'll be quickly swamped. Take photos instead.

Happy Changes: "What's Mine Is Yours"

Wait a minute! You didn't say "I do" to that StairMaster, *Blade Runner* poster, flowered comforter, or collection of Precious Moments figurines—did you? Well, yes, you did. You don't even need a license to move in with a significant other and all his or her stuff. There's a reason that the smoothest transition into sharing your life with someone you love is when you decide on a new place and move into it together. That way the playing field is level and you can negotiate how you want your home furnished. It's a perfect time to use the principles in the section of the book entitled "Assess."

If you are moving into your significant other's established home, don't expect to make sweeping changes or even to bring a lot of your own possessions. The laws of equality don't work here. Your loved one has decorated and arranged things over time to suit himself or herself and will not take kindly to having it all rearranged or decluttered. The transaction will go more smoothly if you recognize this fact of life.

If it is your place being "invaded," understand that now you have to share, particularly in the area of clothes closets, bathroom shelves, bookcases, and kitchen cabinets. You may be seeing things you never expected to find in your living space, and it may not please you. But diplomacy is necessary. An item you feel belongs out on the curb may have great sentimental value for your partner; before you make retching noises, ask about its meaning for him or her.

In 90 percent of all living-together situations, when you try to combine your stuff, there will be too much. Going through this book together and making decisions about the excess, as well as planning your home's mood and functions, can make the transition happier.

Happy Changes: Working at Home

If you're in the process of starting your own business, your first priority will be to get things off the ground and create workable schedules. You'll be throwing yourself into it, working at odd hours or whenever inspiration strikes, and the temptation will be to spread your materials all over your home or apartment. But once you come up for air, it is important to confine all business materials to your home office or garage or wherever your headquarters may be.

I've seen people start out in what they felt was the logical location, only to find that they preferred the light or the mood or the space somewhere else. When that happens, move to the space where you feel most productive, even if it means changing other room functions. No law says the dining room has to remain where it is now if that's the room you like best. But it's better to keep everything in one place, even though it is temporarily cluttered, rather than let the contagion spread throughout your home. It is also easier to find things when there is only one spot they can be.

Happy Changes: "I'm Retired!"

Nobody talks much about the stresses of retirement. But when you leave the workforce permanently, the structure that you functioned under for so many years is gone. Some people cope with this by having part-time work in place or a loved avocation to pursue or volunteer work or travel plans. Yet the fact is that you are closing the door on a significant part of your life, and this has to be acknowledged.

On the other hand, once you have adjusted, retirement is a wonderful time. Retirement is a good time for your home as well. You are now able to make improvements. And since it's a change in lifestyle, it's the perfect time to take a new look at the mood and functions of your home and make sure they are optimal for you.

Traumatic Changes: Crisis Mode

When you find yourself in the midst of a crisis, your physical environment is the least of your concerns. Your ability to cope has been compromised, and your energy is down. You need to keep doing the most important things, such as eating regularly, sleeping enough, and paying bills. If

Household Endangered Species #11
A scarf your great-aunt knit for you. You would wear it if it didn't scratch your neck so badly and was in a color other than lilac, but you're afraid if you actually discard it your aunt's feelings will be hurt.

people offer to help you with any aspect of your life, let them. None of us are superhuman; there's no shame in admitting you can't cope with it all.

There are some fine books that deal extensively with working through life changes. My purpose is to help you in the aftermath, when you are trying to dig out from under and create a new environment. The answer is not to blindly start attacking things and throwing them away. What you need to do is assess your change in circumstances and find a new approach.

Traumatic Changes: When Illness Strikes

You may find everything on hold while you care for an elderly parent, a spouse, or a child who is ill. Once the initial shock is past, you will need to develop new and simplified patterns. You can still think about streamlining and creating a new space, but getting your life in order by creating some routines and having a definite spot for crucial items has to take priority. As long as you take care of your own health and find the joy in being with the people you love, you will come through.

Perhaps you are the one who has suffered a disability or are fighting an illness and need to make adjustments. In that case, it is important to simplify your life as much as possible. If you are having difficulty knowing where to start, I would suggest hiring an expert from the National Association of Professional Organizers (512-206-0151 or napo.net) who can come in and reorganize your space optimally. This person can help you arrange things in the most convenient places and simplify the care you have to give your environment.

Traumatic Changes: Losing Someone Close to You

Before doing anything else, you need to take time to mourn. This time will vary; other people cannot tell you how long it should be.

Only when you have gone through the process will you be able to pick out items of that person that are meaningful to keep, and find good homes for the rest. At first it may seem a betrayal to give anything away. With time you will be able to see that your loved one's things can bless other people who need them, that your memory of the deceased is not dependent on his or her stuff.

Traumatic Changes: Feeling Depressed

The part that depression plays in letting things pile up can be circular. The more of a mess everything is, the worse you feel. The worse you feel, the more powerless you are to do something about it. When you're depressed, you are easily overwhelmed and lack energy to do anything but the usual maintenance, if even that. You're prone to visiting the dark side, telling yourself, "I'll never be able to accomplish anything, so it doesn't really matter." You feel unable to focus long enough to make a plan, much less carry it through. Far from feeling optimistic about the future, you're hanging on to the status quo. Even if you are getting help, the effects are not always immediate.

But besides getting professional help and/or medication, there are one or two simple things you can do. For fifteen minutes a day, just sit by yourself. Remind yourself that life will get better, then imagine the way you want your physical environment to be in the future. Just focus on this one area, although if you start imagining other life changes, let them come. When you're done, write down any ideas in your notebook. It works even when you're not depressed. I've gotten some fascinating ideas, things I had not thought of consciously.

You can also take fifteen minutes—set a timer, if you want—to do something new. Go through your hope chest; add new ideas that you've been accumulating, and weed out what's outdated. Go to your kitchen and pick out several "novelty" utensils or appliances, and put them in a box to give away. Sort through your clothes closet and fill a small bag for the Goodwill. If you want, you can stop when the fifteen minutes are up and consider it a good job. But if your motivation has kicked in, there's no harm to keep going.

Attitude Shifts

The changes we have been discussing are all external events. But they require some changes in your thinking as well.

Recognize That Some Things That Were Important to You in the Past Are Less So Now

Whether the changes you have undergone are happy or traumatic, you will find that your priorities have shifted. These can be as simple as a new mom giving up manicures and perfect nails for a while, a retiree not needing suits and laundered white shirts, or someone recently married getting used to the idea of sharing the closet space. It may go deeper, such as not socializing as part of a couple, cutting down on physical activities, or no longer having a garden. It would be nice if these hangers-on from past priorities would just quietly fall away, but sometimes they need to be given a shove.

One shove they need is physical. There will be a number of things that you'll want to photograph and then find good homes for.

See That What Has Happened Is an Opportunity

Some things that happen in life are truly horrific and can only be endured. Fortunately, most things that happen fall short of that. The theme of the movie *Life Is Beautiful* is that while we cannot change our circumstances, we always have a choice in how to respond to them. Thankfully, we are not imprisoned in a concentration camp, as the film's hero was, and we have broader latitude to change our lives. When people say, about something that was perceived as a negative at the time, "That was the best thing that could have happened to me," they have been able to see new doors open and view new perspectives.

Learn Rather than Regret

While you can learn from your experiences, to continue obsessing about how you caused whatever happened is counterproductive. More than that, it's often inaccurate. To continually feel, "If only I hadn't _____," "It's all my fault that _____," or "I should have been more _____," gets you nowhere that you want to be. The fact is that no one can rewrite history. If you feel you made a mistake, look toward the future to correct it in other ways.

Life Is a Continuum

Somewhere along the line, many people internalized the Hollywood idea "You're only as good as your last picture." That philosophy makes what is happening to you now, who you are right now, the only thing that matters. But life is not a flat oval track. It is a combination of rises and switchbacks, the culmination of our experiences and relationships. If you have experienced a setback, remember that setbacks are usually temporary. Thinking globally—for example, "I'm just a failure. I'll never get anything right!" or "I'll never be happy again!"—isn't helpful. What's more, it isn't true.

Change Is an Inevitable Part of Life

Moving on from the past does not negate it. It does not mean denying it, either. It's helpful to display a picture or memorabilia of how things were before, of you and your former partner, highlights in your career, athletic accomplishments, scenes from happy family times, and so on. Even if things ended unhappily and you feel you have to remove every trace, they'll be in your memory anyway; it is better to celebrate them as part of your life. On the other hand, don't make a shrine that will keep you stuck back there, unable to move on.

To sum it up, as you struggle to regain your equilibrium from life's changes, accept some disorder. With patience, you can make your world even better than it was before!

DANGEROUS PHRASES

- "Nothing good will ever happen again."
- "If only I had _____."
- "I'll *never* be able to get a grip."
- "What's the use?"
- "From here on in it's all downhill."
- "This was a bad idea!"
- "I never should have _____."
- "Why didn't someone tell me?"

STUFF LIST #11

Think about the items you are holding on to from before you retired, had children, moved to a smaller home, or got married, or the things you need to give away from a past relationship. There may be many items that do not work well in your new lifestyle and which you want to give up to make room for new adventures. Ask yourself these two questions:

- "How does this make my life better?"
- "If it were lost in a fire or flood, would I replace it?"

Then list the items here or in your notebook. For disposition, you have a choice of keep, toss, recycle, give away, or sell.

Item	Why I'm Keeping It	Disposition

_____   _____   _____
_____   _____   _____
_____   _____   _____
_____   _____   _____
_____   _____   _____
_____   _____   _____

When you are struggling to let go of items like these in the future, you can tell yourself:

_____

_____

Exercise

Once you have designated outcomes for the things on your list, take a few minutes to mark them following the dot system (see Chapter 2).

Step 2

Assess

12

"But I Don't Know What I'm Doing!"

One of the most resistant clients I ever had was also the most entertaining. Terri was funny and accommodating, and she made great cappuccino. Perhaps because of her cheerful openness, it took me longer than usual to see what her problem really was.

Terri didn't even try to hide her piles of stuff. A fifth grade teacher during the workweek and an avid kayaker, golfer, and political activist the rest of the time, she had obvious interests. Over the couch was a huge, messily taped collage showing her students, past and present. The coffee table was littered with colored paper, stickers, and political pamphlets. Her golf clubs stood beside the front door. Oddly, her kitchen was tidy except for the usual countertop flyers and catalogs, and her bedroom was close to pristine. She *did* have too many clothes jamming her closet. But a second bedroom was set up very neatly as a home office.

"I'm a slob," she said candidly as we returned to the living room. "I'll make us some coffee and we can talk about it."

"What would you like to accomplish?" I asked a few minutes later.

She ran a hand through her close-cropped red hair. "Oh, the usual."

Taking another sip of cappuccino, I said, "Well, the first thing you can do is find a new home for your golf clubs."

But she frowned. "I like having them right beside the door."

And so it went. Terri resisted all attempts to relocate her living room clutter. We worked on her clothes closet instead. The next time we reorganized her kitchen and office.

The Turning Point

Her living room was becoming the elephant no one talked about. Finally I said, "Any thoughts about your living room?"

To my surprise, she walked out of the kitchen. But she returned a few minutes later and hesitantly handed me a magazine photo of a room with a French Country look. There was quilted floral chintz, beautiful polished wood, flowers in vases, and several formal landscape paintings. "Don't laugh," she said.

"I'm not! It's lovely. Have you looked into finding this kind of furniture?"

She looked disconcerted. Then frightened. "It's only a thought," she whispered.

"But it's what you want."

Here's what came out as we talked. Her dream room was very different from the way people saw her. They were comfortable with her disorder because she was "into a million things." She felt that creating the room she wanted would be impossible without the help of a professional decorator, but with so many worthy causes to contribute to, she couldn't justify paying to hire an expert. But what if she tried it herself and made a mess of it? It would be worse to try something ambitious like that and fail than to do nothing at all!

I asked what she liked about the magazine room.

"Well, the furniture looks very comfortable, but it's also elegant. I love the combination of yellow and blue, it reminds me of traveling in southern France. It's so fresh and—uncluttered! And I love flowers. But . . . ," she looked discouraged, "it would cost a fortune to replicate. Even if I could do it."

"You don't have to copy that room exactly to get the same mood. Designer rooms are mostly helpful as triggers. You could find framed pictures and furniture you love, not somebody else's choices. You can't make a mistake when it's your own vision."

She laughed. "You don't know me!"

"But why do you think people will judge what you do?"

"People always judge you."

"And what's the worst thing they can say?"

She thought. "That I'm a pathetic failure who tried to be 'elegant' and couldn't?"

I smiled at her. "We won't let that happen."

After this pep talk, we made plans to work together. Finally motivated, Terri was able to quickly declutter the living room. The collage of students, her classroom projects, and political materials went into her office; the golf clubs and other sports equipment stayed in the trunk of her car. She painted the walls cream and the trim and window frames a Mediterranean blue. After putting an off-white slipcover on the brown-plaid couch, she bought two floral-print chairs with down cushions and even splurged on a beautiful walnut coffee table. Instead of rushing to frame Impressionist prints, she waited and bought two paintings she loved at a local art show.

When you walk into Terri's living room now, your impulse is to settle in and never leave.

I've told Terri's story in detail, both because it exemplifies what we will be working on in the rest of the book and because feelings like hers are at the root of the procrastination from which a lot of people suffer. Not only do we have a gallery of critics from the past in our heads, but we expect that the people we know will be judging our efforts as well. We may not be clear on what we really want ourselves, so we are reluctant to take any steps at all. Making a mistake looms as the worst thing that can happen.

Decorate Where You Are

No, I don't mean in your home. What I mean is, don't be afraid to decorate in accord with the age you are and the interests and experience you have. An interior decorator can come in and give you a beautiful home. But I think it is better for people to do it themselves and learn from the experience. You know what is meaningful to you. Through creating your environment yourself, you learn and are enriched by the process.

When I finished college and was newly married, the rule was to pick one of five or six preordained "styles." The goal was to have complete roomfuls of matching furniture. I chose Early American. One of my first purchases was a maple spinning wheel "planter," about three feet high, that matched the end tables and rocking chair. But this style bore no relation to my life. A year or two later, I discovered auctions and bought banjo clocks, a leather-topped coffee table, and a mahogany secretary, which I painted silver.

I was big on painting things—my bathroom walls were a deep tangerine, the living room an underwater green, the baby's room banana yellow. I went through peacock wicker chairs and chrome-and-glass coffee tables, made tie-dyed curtains and batik pillows. I had a party and let my guests paint the basement walls with Pop Art symbols. There was seemingly no fad too hideous for me not to attempt.

Yet I look back on those days fondly. The spinning wheel with the plastic flower pot in the middle that I never filled still makes me laugh. I learned much more than if I had had a decorator come in and create a beautiful home for me or if I had copied every detail from a magazine.

That is the kind of freedom I want for you. If you enjoy the process and are happy with the result, that's what really counts. In the following chapters, I'll be discussing general principles with you, but like Terri, you'll be creating your own vision.

How did you feel when you read "creating your own vision"? If you felt excited, then you can turn to the next chapter. If you felt a frisson

THE SOUND OF PROCRASTINATION

Although these excuses seem perfectly reasonable and may even contain an element of truth, they're cover-ups for your underlying feelings, many of which are detailed in "Dangerous Phrases."

- "There's no sense in doing much. I'm thinking about moving in a year or two."
- "People think it's fine the way it is now."
- "I'd like to take an interior decorating course first."
- "It will cost more money than we have."
- "My husband/wife doesn't like change."
- "It seems frivolous to spend good money on things for the house."
- "I'd love to do it, but I don't have the time right now."
- "I'm not that interested in decorating; I just want to get rid of some stuff."
- "I like to keep my options open."

of doubt or fear or even panic, let's talk a little about procrastination and perfectionism. Often it comes cloaked in other words, such as the ones detailed in the sidebar "The Sound of Procrastination."

Being the Best

One characteristic of perfectionism is not just wanting to do something the best you can but wanting to do it better than it's ever been done before. That's a tall order, however, especially if it's an area you don't have much experience in. Such expectations can lead to procrastination, either through taking too long to make detailed preparations or by doing nothing at all. If you start feeling pressured by other family members or your own time constraints, you may end up rushing through the job—with the idea that if you had only had longer, it would have been perfect.

Fear of Commitment

If you are afraid of making a disastrous mistake, your redecorating may stay forever in the planning stages. You'll collect lots of beautiful photos and imagine wonderful possibilities but never narrow it down to actually working on a specific room. That way no one will be able to judge your results. In a sense this is similar to the problem of opportunity costs, discussed in Chapter 7. When you settle on a specific plan, you are giving up all the other attractive possibilities that aren't chosen. Your indecision is compounded by the fear that you are choosing the wrong plan.

Forever Unfinished

A variation of being unable to commit to a single plan is getting started and then keeping the room perennially under construction. Some new idea or complication always seems to come along to delay the completion date. But think about it. As long as you are still in the process, you cannot be judged on the outcome. As long as you haven't finished, the element of fantasy is still present, the field of possibilities still wide open. If the thought "As long as we're working in here anyway, we might as well do _____" seems familiar to you, you'll want to guard against falling into this particular trap.

Household Endangered Species #12
The cute purse you bought on impulse for a special occasion, but the special occasion never came.

Attitude Shifts

It takes courage to move ahead and create your own space. Here are some ideas that may help.

No One Lives in Magazine Rooms

The next time you look at a picture in a decorating magazine, mentally take away the flowers, the bowl of fruit, the adorable dog, and the breathtaking scene outside the window (which may not actually be there in real life). What you're left with is a room with furniture not unlike your own. Or maybe not. In an enlightening book by Marjorie Garber, *Sex and Real Estate,* she talks about "propping," which she calls design magazines' "dirty little secret." She explains that propping is "bringing in museum-quality furniture, chenille throws, borrowed art, and masses of flowers to produce the illusion of a beautifully arranged 'home.'"

If you can think of home design magazines as inspirational rather than practical, the way fashion magazines that show extremely expensive outfits are, you can appreciate what they are trying to do. Understand that they are giving you an ultimate, an ideal, a springboard for ideas that you can translate into something that is right for you.

Sometimes magazines show the homes of actual people, albeit very wealthy ones, but even with those rooms you can't always be sure what you are getting. When *In Style* magazine showed Christie Brinkley's summer home in the Hamptons, they brought in furniture from a Bridgehampton antique store and other local venues. Ms. Brinkley liked it so much that she bought the furnishings afterward.

Nothing Is Forever

There are a few things, such as marriage or children, that you take on as a lifelong commitment in good faith. As we know, even the former may not last forever. But there is nothing permanent about home decorating. You can paint your living room or bedroom a different color every six months if you choose. When you bring in something new—say, a painting or a sofa—it affects everything else in the room, which may lead to you making other changes.

My point is that even if you create a room exactly as you want it now, in five years it will have changed—subtly or overtly—into something else. You are continuing to develop, your needs and wants are changing, and it is healthy if your environment grows along with you. I'm not saying this to be discouraging but to reassure you. Even if your worst fears are realized, the dining room color turns out all wrong, and the chest you loved in the showroom turns out to be impractical at home, you are not forever doomed. Rooms can be repainted, and a piece of furniture that does not work in one place is often meant for somewhere else.

Your Home Can Be as Individual as You Are

Just as you have a unique personality, so can your home. In the summer 2006 copy of O at Home, there are stories about two different women: one who creates art using shells and another who always wanted to live in a library. Cathy Jarman and her family live in a fantasyland in which the pièce de résistance is a nine-by-twelve-foot open cabinet, completely shell encrusted, displaying her collection of fish plates and platters by Johnson Brothers. Her work is nationally recognized.

Playwright Marsha Norman, Pulitzer Prize–winning author of 'Night, Mother, lives in a loft with bookshelves forty feet long and sixteen feet high, complete with a library ladder. There are also twenty library lamps and a twenty-foot table that Ms. Norman uses as a desk. As she says, "I didn't want to live in a loft, I wanted to live in a library. . . . This is a place for reading and writing. It is a place to disappear."

When you follow your individual interests and tastes instead of trying to create someone else's ideal, it can take you to wonderful places. If your goal is no more than to create a home that's a haven of soft colors and fabrics, choose the ones that excite you, and you'll end up with a result that you love.

Think of F. Scott Fitzgerald's words: "Start with an individual and you have created a type. Start with a type and you have created . . . nothing." When you follow your individuality and instincts, you can't go wrong.

DANGEROUS PHRASES

- "What if it's a total disaster?"
- "I don't know what I'm doing!"
- "It's better to be safe than sorry."
- "How can I be expected to do a professional job?"
- "I know I'll change my mind."
- "It's not so bad the way it is."
- "I'm thinking about moving in a couple of years."
- "There's no guarantee that it will turn out the way I want it."
- "I'm all thumbs!"
- "Everyone but me seems to know what they want."
- "If I can't do it right, I don't want to do it at all!"

13

Thinking About
Your New Space

When I planned my apartment in the city last year, I had the luxury of starting fresh. Sitting with sheets of graph paper, blank except for the dimensions of the apartment rooms, I went about creating a space that reflected the person I now was and the life I wanted. I thought about how each room would be used, how it would feel, and I made lists of which items should stay in my life and which should go.

Certain things came from our Port Jefferson house because they mean "home": the Navajo rug Tom and I bought years ago on the reservation that now hangs on the wall above the long dining table; several small Oriental rugs and a Tiffany-style lamp that belonged to my parents; family photos, artwork, and the oversized wooden cat that Tom gave me for my birthday one year; a carved oak buffet with a lot of storage space. It was the perfect opportunity for me to choose things I loved that would create the mood I wanted. Tom, who spends more time in Port Jefferson because of his job, has the final say for decorating that house.

Getting in the Mood

Before you make any physical changes, pour yourself a cup of tea or a glass of wine—whatever you find relaxing—and make yourself very comfortable. Then close your eyes and think about how you want your home to feel. Forget about the furniture you already own and the styles in which the rooms are now decorated. Forget about trying to replicate a home you saw in a magazine and admired. What you're honing in on is a feeling.

When I chose a mood for the apartment living room, I wanted it to feel warm, spacious, and welcoming to company, and I wanted it to be filled with creative things. A comfortable, relaxed feeling was more important to me than creating a particular style. As soon as I saw the apartment with its high ceilings and freshly painted white walls, warm honey-colored wood floors, and large, light-filled windows, I knew it would work perfectly.

First Impressions

Someone else, whose dream was to replicate a historic era, might have chosen a space with a lot of dark woodwork, period details, and small, cozy rooms. The architecture can give you a place to begin. Chances are when you chose your house or apartment, there were definite features to which you responded. Think back to what first attracted you, and try and recapture exactly what it was. It may have been subliminal, like the expanse of lawn glimpsed out of French doors. But if it was only half-understood, you may have positioned your sofa with your back to the view because it seemed more logical to be looking into the room, or you may have covered the doors with draperies to conserve heat. If one characteristic you decide that you want is an outdoor feeling, then you know what you have to do.

Another important reason to think back to the things you initially responded to is that at least some of them came from your past experiences, places where, as a child or an adolescent, you felt happy and safe. This may have been your childhood bedroom with its closet passageway leading to other rooms, your grandmother's front porch, or the home of a friend whose parents made you feel special. If you take the time to make these connections, you will also be able to decide how important it is to you to incorporate these feelings into your current environment.

Mood Matters

If you're having trouble conceptualizing a mood, here are some examples that other people have come up with to describe their ideal homes. These are only suggestions—yours will probably be very different!

■ Sheltered and cozy, with country accessories and down-home furniture

■ Peaceful and serene, very Zen, minimal furnishings

■ Exotic and exciting, showing off our travel finds from around the world

■ Warm, with an English cottage feeling—teapots and flowered upholstery

■ Feeling like, but not looking like, the home where I grew up

■ Crisp and sophisticated, with original artwork in lighted alcoves and tailored furniture

■ Nautical, blue and white, with lots of sailing motifs

■ Child-friendly, with lots of nooks and crannies, cute surprises around every corner

■ Showing my love of the theater, with dramatic rooms like stage sets, framed playbills, and a baby grand

■ A Western, pine-scented log cabin to totally kick back in

■ Bringing the outdoors in by large windows and soft greens and blues inside

■ Elegant, with French antiques and paintings in gold frames

■ Like a downtown club, with a pool table, flat-screen TV, black leather furniture

■ Artistic, expressing my work and things my friends have made

■ Feeling like an elegant hotel

Yes, there are people who hire decorators to give their rooms the look of an expensive hotel suite. Perhaps it is an unconscious wish for the uncluttered vacation house feeling. Or they have decided they want to live with the excitement and nonpermanence of simulated travel without the inconvenience of jet lag. Maybe they simply do not want other people judging their personal choices and so find safety in anonymous good taste. The point is, whatever you choose, whatever mood you identify with, will be the right one for you. There is no wrong answer except, possibly, "I haven't a clue," and even that can be fixed.

Mood Problems

Here are some doubts you may be experiencing:

- "I can't think of a thing."
- "When I asked my husband about the feeling he wanted, he said, 'It's fine the way it is!' But it really isn't anything now but a mess."
- "I think I want it to be too many things rolled into one! I can't narrow it down to just one mood."
- "My wife won't get rid of one stick of her family's Victorian furniture. It's crowding out our whole house. Why even worry about mood?"
- "I don't care what it looks like; I just want it to be neat!"
- "I can't think of any style we'd both agree on."
- "I know the mood I want, but I don't know how I'll get it."

It would be wonderful to quickly select a mood and, if you live with other people, have them agree with or even improve on your ideas. Sometimes it works that way. But often it doesn't. If you are stymied by the whole process, the discussion in the sidebar "Why Choosing a Mood for Your Home Is Important" should help.

WHY CHOOSING A MOOD FOR YOUR HOME IS IMPORTANT

1. It is important because you're important. You deserve to have a place that is more than a giant container to hold your stuff.

2. It makes the process of deciding what to keep and what to discard easier. When you are going for a particular look or feeling, knowing what contributes to it helps you make decisions about what to save and what to discard. The focus is taken off the particular item; you won't be obsessing about whether it is too good to get rid of. Instead, you'll be judging it as to whether it works with the larger whole.

A client of mine, George, wanted to turn his garage into a part-time financial consulting office. After thinking about it, he decided that he wanted the mood to be welcoming but professional, minimizing the room's earlier life as a garage. So when he came to a stack of old tires in the corner, he didn't hesitate. Did they help create the professional mood he wanted when people came in? No way. Rather than worrying about whether the tires were still perfectly good or might be used by someone somewhere sometime, he decluttered them instantly because they didn't fit into the larger picture. Their life span was over.

3. It gives you the motivation to keep the room uncluttered. You may think that how a room feels isn't important as long as it's neat. But when it's a place you don't care about, it's going to be that much harder to maintain order. After all, even when it's perfect, an uninspired room still looks—uninspired. A room with meaning and personality glows when it's uncluttered but can still handle a few things out of place.

How to Pick a Mood When You Can't

Having too many ideas and not having any may seem like opposite positions, but the solution for them is the same. Pick up several contemporary decorating books or magazines at the library and page through them. Whenever you see a room that you feel you could live in happily, put a paper slip in to bookmark that page and keep going. After you've gone through several resources, you should have some ideas. Look more closely at the pages you've bookmarked, not to replicate the furnishings, but to pick out the qualities that appeal to you. Hopefully, you'll see a pattern and be able to identify the moods you like. If there are still too many, pick the one that appeals to you most strongly for the living room, and save the rest for the other rooms.

Working It Out with Family Members

Marriage counseling is beyond the scope of this book, but the truth is that many women like to experiment with their environment, an activity that makes many men nervous. Yet just the act of asking your partner for input and being willing to listen can be reassuring to someone who feels anxious about having his world turned upside down. Besides, you're not asking about specific purchases and changes. You're asking about how the other person wants his home to feel: airy or sheltered, relaxed or displaying treasures like a museum, and so on.

Speaking of a museum, even if you live with someone who does not want to relinquish her Victorian furniture collection, you can still select a mood, the strongest feeling you would like the room to convey. Within those confines she may be persuaded to move some of the furniture into other rooms or even into storage, if necessary, and bring in accessories that contribute to a more eclectic feeling.

If you are the one clinging to all your current furnishings or a particular style, ask yourself why it is so hard to let go. You may still be responding to a style that seemed desirable when you were younger. Even if it no longer seems as elegant, it has gained in safety and familiarity. At least it *works*. But consider the possibility that you can move on to something else that not only works but actively brings you joy.

Alternatively, your home may be the way your parents' and grandparents' homes were, especially if you have some of their furniture and accessories. These say stability, tradition, and family to you, even if they may not have the same meaning for the people you live with. But at least ask yourself these questions: Am I moving ahead in my life and interests as quickly as I want? Is my environment holding me back in subtle ways? Have I let things get into a cluttered state because my home no longer excites me? Finally, ask yourself if you could do with fewer of these items. It's too easy to slip into an all-or-nothing mentality.

Frankly, it would be unusual if your priorities, your needs for nurturing, and the feeling you want your environment to have had not changed in twenty or thirty years.

Don't Think of It as Decorating

If you look at the room you're currently sitting in and shudder, take heart. You may be one of the people who lament, "I'm terrible at decorating! I just can't picture how anything is going to look." But this isn't decorating in the traditional sense. We are going slowly, step-by-step, eliminating everything that doesn't make a contribution, with the aim of creating a home that's satisfying to you. The room may stay a work in progress for a while as you furnish it only with

Household Endangered Species #13
Lampshades from lamps you no longer own but which might work on a light that comes without its own shade in the future.

what you love and need and retain only items from the past that give meaning to who you are.

Your taste is the most important decorating component. When I watch room makeovers on television, I sometimes wonder how long-lasting they will be. What really happens when decorators bring in new and charming accessories that support a theme but have no personal connection to the homeowners? Do the homeowners come to love these items that they didn't choose and have no personal history with? Or do they soon replace the items with familiar things? In order to nurture us, our homes need a blend of the personal and the purchased.

As for mistakes—and we all make them—they are inevitable, but most are easily corrected. When I was planning my apartment living room, I decided to flank the large window with two tall white bookcases, one on each side, as if they had been built in. On paper it looked fine. But when the bookcases arrived and I put them in place, I was dismayed to find that together they shortened the room and gave an unpleasant, claustrophobic feeling—not what I could have predicted and certainly not what I wanted. So instead of my original plan, I hung a large picture on the opposite side of the window and moved the second bookcase to another part of the room.

MOOD RECAP

1. Remember why you are redecorating. Not for a photo shoot in *Architectural Digest* or *House Beautiful*. Not for the admiration of your friends, family, or strangers, though if your authenticity shines through, they will be impressed. Naturally, you want a beautiful home. But pleasing other people is not your primary goal.

2. Forget complicated arrangements, at least in the beginning. I mean those magazine vignettes showing an occasional table holding an orchid, a sterling-framed photograph, and two polished beach stones. Yes, they can look charming. But you don't need a showplace—you want a home that real people can use. These decorative clusters have to be kept just so and can be thrown off kilter by a pair of reading glasses or a used coffee cup placed nearby.

3. Make use of things that energize a space. Fresh flowers and plants, candles, decorative pillows, interesting artwork, small dishes of candy—all of these lift people's spirits. So do sentimental items that hold happy memories. No matter what your theme is, Manhattan penthouse or Western ranch, you can find accessories that appeal to the senses.

4. When planning a new area, don't fill it up completely, especially if you don't love that many of your current possessions. It's important to deliberately allow some empty spaces for new and better items and fresh interests. Feng shui emphasizes both the principle of leaving enough room for the chi (good energy) to flow and the importance of keeping your belongings current.

5. One reason I suggest planning the rooms before discarding anything is because pieces that don't seem to work in one room any longer can take on new life somewhere else. Some of my furniture, especially smaller pieces, has been in several different rooms over time. Furniture can be cut down, repainted, or used just as it is, so think twice before discarding a piece that you like. Lamps, chests, chairs, artwork, and accessories are especially versatile.

6. If you have collections displayed in the living room, make sure they actively please you when you see them and that they haven't "died." If necessary, look at Chapter 10 (on collections) again.

7. Prime the pump by looking at some decorating books. You won't be looking for rooms to replicate; you'll just be looking at what's possible, to catch the spirit. Whenever I plan to make changes, I like to leaf through various books for inspiration, including *Fantasy Rooms* by Laurence Llewelyn-Bowen, *Breaking the Rules* by Christy Ferer, and *Artists' Interiors: Creative Spaces, Inspired Living* by Laurie E. Dickson. Am I going to re-create my dining room as an Egyptian tomb? Not likely. But seeing one in *Fantasy Rooms* may open my thoughts in a new direction.

Deciding Function

Before I became a professional organizer and home designer, when I thought about the purpose of rooms in my own house, I would feel paralyzed. Perhaps I believed myself too much of a free spirit and resisted being told what I should be doing where. Perhaps it just seemed too hard. But if you find yourself resisting this part of the process, I can sympathize.

There is a gap, too, between the ideal images we have and the way life actually unfolds. You may imagine yourself in your living room or den, scented candles glowing, music playing softly, as you snuggle up with a great book. Only—it never seems to happen. Or you picture the whole family grouped around contentedly, involved in compatible pursuits or playing a game together. Except—Dad is in the home office catching up on e-mail, Mom is on the phone, and the kids are either watching TV, doing homework, or in their rooms instant messaging. It's enough to make you wonder, "Why bother?"

But look at it this way: if you choose the functions you would like for each room and create an area that supports them, there's a much greater chance that you or your family will use the space as intended. If you leave it as it is, there's little chance of it happening at all.

With these things in mind and your mood chosen, it's time to create your mission statement.

Mission Statements

The mission statement is a concept that I strongly encourage my workshop audiences to use. When I first began decluttering my own home years ago, my mission statement was as follows:

> I want my home to have that vacation house feeling. So I will find a place for everything and keep only what I love and use.

At that point, I was focused on decluttering and simplifying.

The most helpful thing about a mission statement is its power to sustain you. For me it was the bright light shining just up ahead, the outcome that I knew I wanted. I had experienced the vacation feeling, if only briefly, and the memory carried me through all those discouraging times when I felt, "This is hopeless! No one is able to live that way."

I mentioned my client George, who was able to quickly get rid of the old tires he had been saving. When we worked together, his mission statement was as follows:

> I want to turn the garage from hell into an office for a part-time financial consulting business. So I will need to clear out all the junk and furnish the room in a way that gives me confidence and makes my clients feel secure about my abilities.

The last time I heard from him, his business had taken off.

An art teacher I worked with wrote this as her mission statement:

I want my home to represent *me*, with room for new energy to come into my life. So I will get rid of everything that is keeping me stuck in the past and replace it with what is important to me now.

One of the things she did was to turn what had been a junk room into a meditation sanctuary. Then she fell in love, got engaged, and moved to California.

When you write your home mission statement, you can be as specific as you want. You will be writing one for each of the rooms in your home, however, so don't feel that you have to include all your plans here. I have begun the mission statements that follow with "I." If you live with other people, you can either do them together or each write your own and then compare notes.

Think back on the mood and functions you chose, and then write your mission statement here or in your notebook.

Home Mission Statement
I want my home to

_____

_____

_____

So I will

_____

_____

_____

14

The Living Room

To me, the living room is the most fascinating space in the house. It is the first place that outsiders see when they come into your home. Even more important, it is the first room that you see when you open your front door at the end of a grueling day. You want to walk into a place that makes you feel comfortable and uplifted and that lets you know you are *home*.

If, instead, you come in and see an unloved couch you bought because it could be delivered right away, catalogs and newspapers tossed on the chairs, the dry cleaning you keep forgetting to take, a nonworking lamp, and someone's coat dropped on the floor, your mood is not going to soar. Chances are that you'll only be happy that no company is walking in behind you.

How we get from "Eek!" to "Ahh" is not complicated, but it takes some thought and planning. It means deciding how you want the room to look, function, and feel and writing a mission statement to that effect. It means choosing which things will stay and which things have to go, as well as deciding what, if anything, you need to add. I've placed the actual disposing of items in the final section so that you do not duplicate your efforts in, say, having a garage sale. But trash can be disposed of as you go along.

A THOUGHT ON "DONATING"

Speaking of trash, psychologist Martha Beck points out, "Believing you must donate or sell your clutter is another relic of the days when people suffered from scarcity. The poor aren't a junkyard substitute. . . . Give away items only if they are in good condition." So unless something is genuinely useful or attractive, don't add it to a charity's clutter. You can escort it right out the door to the curb instead.

How you use your living room may depend on whether you also have a family room or great room. If you do, you will use your living room differently and think of it more for entertaining and display—although if you live with other people and the television is always on, you may find yourself retreating to a space in the living room where you can listen to music or read quietly.

Living Room Rules

Before you choose your mood and function, there are some important things to know.

1. Whether you live by yourself or with other people, everyone needs a comfort zone that is his or hers alone. It may be a chair or loveseat, a window seat or one end of a sofa. But it has to be comfortable, have good lighting, and pull you in. My friend Penny stipulates that her chair has to have her things permanently around it—the magazines and books she wants to read, her knitting, and a pad on which to jot ideas. "If it's in a closet two rooms away, I won't bother to get it," she points out.

When I was at a spa last year, the hot topic among the women was about buying the perfect chair—for themselves. The styles they chose varied from Stickley to French Country, but there seemed to be a preference for matching ottomans, which would create a recliner effect. Women who seemed otherwise frugal had no difficulty paying a premium for a chair that would satisfy their needs.

2. In the interest of serenity, certain offenders should be banned from the living room. These can include mail, coats, briefcases, school bags and sporting goods, sloppy snacks, toys left out (especially if you have a den or family room), or anything else that creates instant clutter. Make sure, however, that you have provided a viable alternative for those things somewhere else in your home.

3. Have at least one thing in the room that excites you. This can be anything from artwork to an heirloom rug, a favorite chair, a lamp, a vacation souvenir, a displayed collection, a special photograph, a baby grand piano, or an orange tree. Its primary purpose isn't for the admiration of other people but for you to feel happy to have it near you. Ideally, you will have many things you feel this way about, but you should have at least one of them in every room.

4. Decide what your focal point is. Simply put, this is what your eye notices first when you come into a room. In many homes it's the fireplace or the painting over the couch or a wonderful window view. You will have other places of interest in the room that will be noticed more gradually, but your primary focal point is the one you want to play up. If you're having a problem figuring out what it is, go outside and come back in as if you'd never seen your living room before. What do you see first? Your fireplace, by default? The large-screen TV with a stack of tottering catalogs on top? Decide what you want to have noticed first in the room, and then situate everything else with that in mind.

5. Not everyone can be the star. If you have dramatic artwork and accessories, they'll do better with furniture that is upholstered in neutrals. The same goes for lamps that aren't meant to be your focal point. It's a temptation to buy only items that are eye-catching and

unique, but unless you know how to create that beautifully chaotic look, it just gets confusing. In the same way, your eye needs some blank spaces to rest on. You don't need artwork hanging on all four walls.

6. The most active image of a living room is people sitting around comfortably, having a conversation. If you have two couches, or a couch and a loveseat, or a couch and two chairs, they should face each other close enough for people to have a conversation without yelling. Some decorators advocate doing away with all couches since usually only two people will sit on one, but I find a loveseat too short for a good nap.

Deciding on a Mood

In Chapter 13 you chose the mood you wanted for your home. It's now time to make the same decision for your living room. Look back at what you wrote down for your home mission statement, "I want my home to . . . ," since it will remind you of your larger goals. You can decorate every room in your house or apartment with a different theme if you choose; just make sure it reflects how you want your home to *feel*. If you wrote down "warm and friendly," a Zen living room done in blacks, whites, and grays with a sense of restraint won't give you the mood you want. Yet if you hang a colorful kimono on the wall as your focal point, place a tea set invitingly on the coffee table, and add comfortable seating with bright cushions, you *will* have a room that meets your criteria.

Mood is not the same thing as style, although one affects the other. The stronger the style you choose, the more it will reference back to a particular geographic area or historic time. When you hear the term *Victorian* or *Swedish Modern* or *1950s*, definite images come to mind. It can be exhilarating to research and create a time or place you feel drawn to; just don't lose sight of the way you want the room to function.

Some styles and moods are more compatible than others—you'll have to work harder to pair "cute and cozy" with sophisticated 1930s decor, for instance—but theoretically anything is possible.

Taking a Poll

Go into your living room and sit down in your favorite place—or places, if you are doing this with your partner or family. Then look around you and write down the following here or in your notebook:

Five things in this room that I love and want to keep:

_____

_____

_____

_____

_____

Five things in this room that I hate or feel should be changed:

_____

_____

_____

_____

_____

You may get some interesting reactions, including your own. Following are some examples:

- "I don't know why we ever got it; I hate beanbag chairs!"
- "One thing I could never part with is my grandparents' Bible."
- "Those dead plants are pathetic."
- "The computer looks out of place in here."

- "The bookshelves are too cluttered with stuff. They should only have books on them."
- "I love that old trunk. It reminds me of faraway places."

And so on. Hopefully, if you're doing this exercise with other people, there will be some consensus. But this is only the beginning. Next, you need to factor in how the room is going to be used. Look at some of the possible functions in the sidebar "The Living Room as a Place for . . ."

THE LIVING ROOM AS A PLACE FOR . . .

Your living room can be used in a number of different ways. It can be a place for any of the following:

- Entertaining company
- Gathering to read aloud
- Curling up with music and a book
- Watching TV and DVDs
- Holding meetings
- Napping
- Displaying art and your collections
- Daydreaming
- Playing the piano
- Relaxing as a family
- Paying bills
- Working on hobbies
- Storing books
- Playing games
- Accommodating overnight guests

Putting It Together

Think about the mood you want and the way you want your living room to function. If you want to use your living room to store and display books, for instance, you may need more shelving; if it is to be used for overnight guests, you'll want to have a sofa bed or a comfortable place to put an inflatable mattress. If you plan to pay bills here, you'll want a desk or one of those kidney-shaped wooden lap desks

Household Endangered Species #14
Even though no one in the family smokes and you don't allow smoking inside your house, you are holding on to your ashtrays just in case.

sold by Levenger. The one thing that is not negotiable is comfortable seating for each family member.

Living Room Mission Statement

I want my living room to

_____

_____

_____

So I will

_____

_____

_____

Taking Action

Go into your living room. You will be looking at what's there and dividing it into three categories, either mentally or written down in your notebook: (1) things that you love and want to keep, (2) things that you don't care that much about but are necessary at least for the moment, and (3) things that don't work and have to go.

With furnishings that fall into the third category, use the dot system described in Chapter 2. If the yellow-dot items can fit in a trash bag or recycling container, you can get rid of them right away.

Next, assess whatever you need to do or buy, such as painting the walls, putting up more shelves, or buying furniture or accessories. Write them down here or in your notebook.

_____

_____

_____

_____

_____

15

Dining in Style

Dining rooms have fallen somewhat out of favor, but to me they're magical places. There is something about the combination of food, wine, candlelight, and conversation in a room dedicated to that purpose that inspires wonderful evenings. Remarks seem wittier, insights more profound, the feelings expressed truer. Think back to memorable dinners, either in a restaurant or in someone's home, and try to dissect the magic. The food and company were crucial, but the ambience also played a part.

You may be at the busiest stage in your life, where giving a dinner party seems like a pipe dream. But eating in a dining room or dining area with family members or even alone fosters a tendency to slow down and appreciate what you are doing. For us, it was the time of the day to all be together. When Andy and his friends were teenagers, it seemed even more important to have dinner together every night. Breakfast was a frantic affair, and no one was home for lunch, so dinner was the one chance to talk, laugh, and find out what was really going on.

This is not to say that the dining room cannot have a dual purpose and other uses. If space is at a premium, it makes sense to use the room for other activities. Some combinations lend themselves to the mystique. I've had wonderful times in rooms that doubled as libraries, surrounded by books and leather furniture, and in rooms that were artists' studios during the day. What isn't as successful is a room that has office furniture, computers, and telephones in view. Perhaps it is simply a throwback to too many people having eaten too many quick lunches at their desks, but even family members don't tend to linger in an office setting. If the space is used that way, try and stow the business items away at mealtime.

Household Endangered Species #15
A nice collection of doorknobs that you saved when the doors were replaced by new ones. You never know . . .

Unlike the living room, the needs of your dining room or dining area are fewer but more definite: a table, comfortable chairs, dishes and flatware, a china cabinet or buffet, interesting lighting and ambience, and appropriate art. Actually, having storage in the dining room isn't mandatory, although it makes things more convenient.

Table Manners

Round tables are wonderful for conversation and a sense of well-being, but sometimes they don't fit your space. In my apartment, what works best is a long, fairly narrow wooden table that seats up to eight. Upholstered chairs are no doubt the most comfortable, but people seem to do well enough on cane, rattan, or molded wooden seats. If you can, avoid putting company on folding chairs or backless benches. It's easy to feel discriminated against if you are the one without the real chair.

Now is the logical time to go through your table linens. Many people have piles of them yet scramble around when it's time to choose a tablecloth for company. A surprising number of the tablecloths we are holding on to have permanent stains, are the wrong color for our china, or are the wrong size for the table. A friend of mine, seeing that all the tablecloth sizes were on sale for the same price, decided she might as well take advantage of the bargain and bought the largest. Unfortunately, the rectangular cloth reaches the floor. "It looks like a draped coffin," she laments. "When I put the flower arrangement on top, all it needs is a framed photo and a Bible."

For most of my adult life, I had a round oak table with leaves. So why did I have a collection of rectangular and square tablecloths? Several of them, lovely but impractical, had been inherited. Others I bought myself when I wanted a particular color that wasn't available in oblong. Some of the round and oblong cloths I *did* own had those telltale darker patches that indicate where a stain has been. You may find you have similar misfits, as well as tablecloths in holiday colors that clash with your dishes. Place mats, sad to say, have a short life before they start looking tatty.

You may end up with only one or two tablecloths that you like and can actually use, but if you need another, you can get no-iron blends at reasonable prices. (Be sure to measure your table first.) The heirlooms and lace can go to a consignment shop or be used as window swags. Don't even bother giving linens that are stained or worn limp to charity. Just say good-bye.

What's in That Drawer?

Dining room furniture sets used to come with matching china cabinets, buffets, and other storage pieces. If you own that type of older furniture, it's time to take a look at what's hiding behind closed doors. There may be a wealth of household endangered species in hiding, everything from inherited sets of china you never use to those hand-me-down serving pieces for appetizers, made of mahogany, hammered metal, or ceramic sections. Most of them have two main characteristics: they're ugly and they're indestructible. If you're not using them, let them go.

You'll also come across orphaned dinnerware and glassware, as well as other pieces that are the remains of sets. But unless you plan to make a statement by using them at your next dinner party, it's time to say good-bye. Along with them can go pieces where the silver plate has rubbed away; sterling salt shakers whose tops have become corroded; chipped fake fruit; novelty trivets that don't go with your china; half-burned tapers; empty miniature liquor bottles; holiday table decorations that look tired; and all the gift or souvenir items that have collected here, from the cute Amish boy and girl salt shakers to the White House hot plate tile.

You may also uncover pieces that were wedding gifts that you have never had occasion to use and probably never will, everything from marble cheese slabs to silver trays to tiny crystal salt and pepper shakers. How about wine carafes, strange candlesticks, chafing dishes, hideous ashtrays, and seafood-eating sets? You've already thanked the giver. Now is the time to find them a more appreciative home.

Then there are all those other things that have nothing to do with dining that somehow found their way here. If you still need any of these items, put them where they belong. But chances are you didn't miss them and they ended up here because they had nowhere else to go. Although I don't always advocate emptying a drawer or cabinet completely, in this case it's a good idea. Put back only what you are *sure* you'll use. It will give you a psychological lift to look into a cabinet or drawer and see only items that match and that you are happy to have.

Light and Sound

If your space is a dining room, you no doubt have some kind of overhead lamp or chandelier. Put it on a dimmer if it isn't already. If your dining area is part of a larger room, try to have lighting specific to the area that signals what the space is used for. It's also nice to be able to hear music while you eat. If the living room is too far away from the dining area, consider bringing an extra set of speakers into the room.

Appropriate Art

I'm always fascinated by the pictures people hang on their walls, not just in the dining room but everywhere. I'm not talking about good or bad art; I mean the content. Battlefields, storms at sea, unhappy faces, a dead rabbit in a still life. My parents had a Victorian fire screen that showed a little girl sprawled on jutting rocks beside her St. Bernard rescuer; it was hard to believe from her pallid face and closed eyes that she was not permanently drowned.

Inherited art is often dark or stern, or it reflects a past ethos that you don't want to get stuck in. It may have had meaning for your parents or grandparents, but if you don't connect with it or it doesn't raise your spirits, it should go.

People purchase art for many reasons. Sometimes they select art that reflects a crisis they are going through at the moment, in colors that reflect a melancholy or violent mood. The trauma passes, but the unsettling art lingers on. Or people will select a print because it is dramatic or well known. But many dramatic paintings center around a crisis. Someone getting skewered in battle or lost at sea or a bull being gored may not be what you want to focus on while eating.

Art Patrol

Although we are talking about the dining area, now is also a good time to take ten or fifteen minutes to walk through your home and see what art you have displayed. Look at each piece, and think about what it represents to you and how it makes you feel. A picturesque photograph of a door ajar can either mean opportunity beckoning or an opportunity for escape. Photographs of family and good friends are mood enhancers, but make sure they are large enough and are displayed where you can see them. A group of tiny framed photos on a tabletop or bookshelf can quickly become just clutter.

More than many other things, art has a shelf life as we change and develop. When I was helping Margaret renovate her home office, we came across a treasure trove of forgotten posters, including one showing a younger group of Rolling Stones. Laughing, we showed the posters to her daughters, who claimed them for their own. You may have similar posters of humor or allegiance still hanging on your walls or find that earlier interests like the Three Stooges or *The Wizard of Oz* don't do it for you anymore. Take a photo if you have to, but then say good-bye.

So what kind of art should you have? The answer is, anything that inspires you now. If a sculpture of two idealized shapes intertwined or a Thomas Kinkade village scene lifts your mood, go for it. Paintings of clowns set some people's teeth on edge, but you might love them. What you choose does not have to be overtly happy. Landscapes, artistic photographs, textiles, folk art, rugs, abstract paintings in satisfying colors, and vintage travel posters can all contribute to raising your spirits. And they beat drowning sailors by a mile.

Fantasy Meals

You can have fun with a dining room, picking a theme and elaborating on it. Unlike other rooms in the house, it can be confined to the table setting and one or two accessories and does not have to represent a major financial commitment. You can create anything from a Mexican fiesta to a French bistro or an English tearoom. If you're more ambitious, you can frame and hang posters from Broadway shows and turn the dining room into a nightspot. Exotic prints used as tablecloths, colorful tiles for hot plates, and gauzy drapery will let you dine in a Moroccan tent. Using lots of candles can create many different moods. A benefit of creating a larger or different world, even if it seems a little silly to you, is that it encourages people to move out of their accustomed roles and into other realms of possibility.

Dining Room Checklist

These are the basics for your dining room:

- A large enough table and comfortable chairs
- Art that adds to the mood
- Adequate storage holding only dining room dishes, silverware, serving pieces, and table linens that you actually use
- Good lighting

Dining Room Mission Statement

I want my dining room to

_____

_____

_____

So I will

_____

_____

_____

Taking Action

Look around your dining room, thinking of the way you want it to be. Decide what is in here that supports your mood and function and will stay. With items you decide have to go but are still good, use the dot system from Chapter 2.

Next, assess anything you need to do or buy, such as painting the walls or purchasing new furniture or accessories, and write them down here or in your notebook.

_____

_____

_____

16

Anyone in the Kitchen?

People love other people's kitchens. Given the choice of sitting on a comfortable living room sofa or crowding into a steamy kitchen during a party, it's no contest—I've had to physically move people so I could get something out of the oven. The kitchen is the original comfort zone. Nobody cares whether it holds a professional six-burner range or an older stove that isn't even self-cleaning, a refrigerator that makes ice cubes or one that just keeps beer cold. In fact, older, homelier appliances and cabinets can add a feeling of welcome to your kitchen.

When I was checking out the newest kitchen information, I was interested in a comment made by Johnny Grey, a British kitchen designer and author of *Kitchen, a Home Design Workbook*:

> I recall with great affection the small, chaotic family kitchen in our London house where my mother cooked for the seven of us, and where we ate most meals. Although the kitchen was very cramped, low-ceilinged and dark . . . mealtimes were memorable for their animated conversation and laughter. To my mind, too few kitchens seem to be able to combine successful planning with the warm atmosphere I remember from my childhood.

Yet despite all our state-of-the-art equipment, this does not seem to be where we are headed. It has been suggested that the fancier our kitchens are, the less time we spend in them. But I think that's true across the board. Pizza, Chinese takeout, frozen entrées, and other convenience foods are part of our daily diet. Working parents fix quick meals using basic equipment. It is estimated that as Americans we eat a quarter of our meals in restaurants and that two-thirds of what we *do* eat at home is takeout or frozen and prepared by someone else.

Room to Dream

Few people believe that designer kitchens and state-of-the-art equipment are for heavy cooking anyway. Rather, having such a kitchen shows that you appreciate fine food and know what it takes to prepare it—and that you would do it yourself if you only had the time. Such kitchens may reflect our hopes and aspirations, our dreams of the gourmet cooking we will do in the future.

Appliance manufacturers, dependent on steady sales, help us dream by creating new and ever better features. As Winfred Gallagher points out in *House Thinking,* "Many domestic goods and services, from pasta makers to gardeners, imply that our homes should compete with four-star hotels and restaurants. Far from adding to our leisure time, 'labor-saving' bread mixers and floor waxers can devour it."

There are other reasons for professionally equipped kitchens. When we outfit them with granite countertops, expensive appliances, temperature-controlled wine cellars, and the like, we may be doing it because it is expected of us as part of "living the good life."

Just Say No

Although this is treading on sacred earth, I believe that the majority of expensive kitchen renovations are unnecessary. The pressure to expand and update is so relentless, the expectation that you will spend $50,000 at least once to remodel your kitchen is so commonly accepted, that we sometimes forget how uncommon it is in the rest of the world. We forget that we can make our own changes for far less money or that we can decide the room has its own charm and do nothing at all.

The rationale most commonly given for extensive kitchen remodeling is that it will improve the resale value of your home. You probably will get your money back if you sell within five years, but it doesn't always matter. My friends Brenda and Fred recently sold their Long Island home to move to Port Townsend, Washington. They decided that they would not make any expensive repairs or do any remodeling, that their Victorian home could be sold as a fixer-upper if need be. An English family, transferred to New York, saw it and loved it just as it was.

Our "outdated" kitchen in Port Jefferson works fine. But what I yearned for was a sunroom, so I created one from a nine-by-nine-foot windowless, charmless pantry. I did the demolition work of the pantry closet, which had shelves to the ceiling, painted the walls, and tiled the floor with twelve-inch squares that looked like stone. An electrician replaced the overhead light, and professionals cut an opening and put in a large window and French door overlooking the back garden. With a colorful Italian tile table that seats five, plants, and shelves for cookbooks and art, it is a magical retreat for a total price of $3,000.

The other cost was giving up the storage pantry, which meant I needed new places for what had been on the shelves. I realized that the tall, narrow broom closet next to the stove was taking up prime space, so I added shelves to it for food storage. Otherwise, it was a good opportunity to give away everything from novelty baking tins to the vases and baskets from flower arrangements. Because I had a plan, I was motivated to get rid of things that were just taking up space in the pantry and kitchen.

My mission statement was "I want a beautiful sunroom off the kitchen. So I will create one and find permanent homes for the displaced items." I came face-to-face with the fact that I would never be making madeleines in that charming, fluted pan and that saving the shells and special plates for escargot was a luxury I couldn't afford. A number of other items got downsized as well. It seemed a small price to pay.

Small Changes

So what does all this have to do with your kitchen? In part, to help convince you that you can have a wonderful and functional kitchen without going to great expense. Often, changing only one or two things will make you happier with the room. Look around your kitchen and see what makes you cringe. For me it was the old scratched aluminum sink that seemed to laugh mockingly when I tried to polish it. So I replaced it with a white porcelain insert and new faucet I found at a home improvement store. It became my favorite thing in the kitchen.

Your kitchen may need no more than new flooring, fresh paint on the walls, or accessories that please you, if that. If any of your appliances work poorly, they should be replaced. Changing the artwork or the cabinet hardware can make a difference. Or the room may need nothing but clearing some things out and reorganizing what's left. First, though, there's the matter of deciding on function and mood.

Name That Function!

In the beginning of the chapter, I talked about how people like to congregate in kitchens for the warmth, company, and comfort of food. You may want to encourage this by adding stools to a counter or adding a table and chairs. If you have room, you can even add a couch or other seating. Check the suggestions in the sidebar "Kitchen Identification" for further possibilities.

KITCHEN IDENTIFICATION

Most rooms that are kitchens are involved with the preparation and serving of food, but here are some additional functions you might want to consider:

- Greenhouse
- Reading nook
- Homework area
- Sunroom
- Bill-paying center
- Dining area
- Craft studio
- Gathering place
- Experimental cooking lab
- Aviary or aquarium area
- Place to display antique kitchenware or glassware
- Canning and preserving center
- Anything else you want

Function and Mood

You need to be clear on how you want your kitchen used so that it does not become a catchall for mail, tools, backpacks, library books, and so on. Think about what makes sense for your lifestyle, and consult with other family members, if appropriate. What you decide will be part of your mission statement.

If you feel dissatisfied with your kitchen but aren't sure why, here's another exercise to do yourself or with anyone you live with. Go to your kitchen, then write the following here or in your notebook:

What I like most about this kitchen:

_____

_____

_____

_____

What I dislike or would like to change about this kitchen:

_____

_____

_____

_____

Clearing Out

No matter what you decide your kitchen needs, reducing the volume is a good place to start. Although I don't suggest doing this in every room, the best way to streamline your kitchen is by removing *everything*—from coffee mugs to cans of soup to paper napkins to colanders. Before you do this, decide if you want to line the shelves. If you do, buy a roll of coated wallpaper or shelf paper in advance. If you don't already have drawer inserts for silverware and utensils, purchase those at Home Depot, Target, or another housewares store. Also gather lots of empty cartons and a box of large trash bags.

Empty the cabinets, cupboards, drawers, and counters, and put everything just outside the kitchen if you can. Then clean the interior storage spaces thoroughly and measure and line shelves and drawer bottoms. When you are ready, start by first putting back only the things you've used in the last month: the mugs and glasses you actually drank from, the pots and pans you used in cooking. Your everyday dishes, flatware, cookware, utensils, and cups should be stored in the easiest places to reach. Other items that you do use but less frequently, such as a turkey roaster or rolling pin, can go in the deeper parts of your cabinets. Replace the food you know you will eat, the spices you will use.

A Word About Counters

People like to complain that they don't have enough counter space. But unless you're preparing a banquet, just how much room do you need? If you keep your counters clear except for the equipment you use every day—a toaster or toaster oven, microwave oven, and coffee maker—there's enough room to chop vegetables and prepare dishes in even the tiniest kitchen. With the extra space you now have from clearing out the drawers and cabinets, you'll be able to store away anything else—and find it when its turn has come.

Specialty Items

One group of items you will come across are the pieces of novelty cookware, bought because you thought the special cooking pieces would improve your eating experience or be fun to try or help you master a new challenge. But you may not have realized what was involved. Just as growing your own tomatoes is not about saving money, making your own pizza or pasta or soft-serve ice cream or carrot juice

Household Endangered Species #16
A complete service of china with twenty-four place settings, which you inherited. It takes up most of your hutch and you rarely use it because you don't like the pattern, but it's a family heirloom.

is neither time-saving nor economical. After participating in these labor-intensive activities a few times, you may be ready to retire the equipment.

Leftovers

After a while you will be left with an assortment of implements, serving pieces, odd pots, shopping bags, miscellaneous metal parts, specialty glassware, and so on. Don't put these back! The household endangered species that no one can realistically use—and that includes leftover pieces from dish sets, novelty mugs, weird condiments or seasonings, used birthday candles, packets of soy sauce, scorched pot holders—should be put in the trash bags, along with any foodstuffs that seem old. Include torn-out recipes, stained cookbooks, and anything dented or cracked.

Be selective about any food you know you will not use, and plan to give it to your local food bank. A three-year-old can of wild mushroom soup in sherry sauce should be disposed of quietly, not passed on.

Next, look at things that are still useful but which *you* don't use. These can be anything from the fondue set you bought when fondue seemed to be making a comeback, an electric kettle, multiple serving trays, cake pans in the shape of animals, old corkscrews when you now own a rabbit style, nutcrackers, cookie cutters, and specialty dessert plates.

The last group to consider are the items that are still "perfectly good," from bent-pronged corn-on-the-cob holders to fat rubber bands. Go back into your kitchen, open drawers and cabinets, and notice how spacious and convenient everything looks and feels. Do you really want to give that up? Think easy living. Think vacation house feeling.

Taking Action

After you have put as much as possible in the trash bags, get out your dots. (See Chapter 2.)

Kitchen Mission Statement

Once you decide on the mood and function and the things you would like to change, you will have a direction and can write the mission statement for your kitchen.

I want my kitchen to

_____

_____

_____

So I will

_____

_____

_____

Finally, assess what you need to do or buy, such as painting the walls or purchasing new furniture or accessories. Write them down here or in your notebook.

_____

_____

_____

17

Sleeping Through the Night

Think back to the most wonderful bedroom you ever slept in. Take a moment and run through childhood experiences, hotel stays, bed-and-breakfast visits, the homes of friends. If you can picture a particular place, that's wonderful. When I tried to do this, what I finally came up with was a composite.

I see a high, four-poster queen-sized bed with a puffy white comforter and a mattress perfect for deep sleeping. Across the room French doors open onto a balcony overlooking the sea. Inside the room is a very comfortable chair next to a small glass-topped table, a perfect area for having coffee or reading. Off the bedroom is a light-filled bathroom with a deep tub. In the bathroom are also fresh flowers and little soaps in the shapes of shells and starfish. The overwhelming sense is calm and quiet.

Your fantasy bedroom was probably quite different from mine; maybe it had a fireplace or overtly sensual velvets and deep reds. It may have had a canopy bed and gauzy netting or been done in a Western style with dream catchers and a skylight overhead, allowing you to lie in bed and see the stars. If you yearn for Asian simplicity, there was probably a low mattress, tatami screens, and soothing colors. One client wanted to re-create a room from a childhood beach cottage, with a white iron bed, homemade quilt, and little else in the room.

But the bedroom is a place where you can create whatever fantasy you want for yourself, or for you and your partner, a place that you never have to show to anyone if you don't want to. It's a place to feel sensual, to relax, and let time slow. As feng shui expert Terah Kathryn Collins puts it, "Bedrooms are meant for sleeping, reading, reflecting, romancing, and recharging your batteries—a perfect antidote for a busy, stressful day. . . . A cozy, sensual bedroom atmosphere invites complete rest and rejuvenation."

To that I would add only that the bedroom is generally used for storing your clothes and getting dressed as well.

Counting Electric Sheep

After you've remembered your favorite bedroom or created one, think about what wasn't there. My fantasy bedroom did not include a television set, a computer, a desk, exercise equipment, or a wet bar. If there was a clothes closet, it did not dominate the room.

When I attended a weekend conference and shared a room with a friend, she woke up the next morning and said enthusiastically, "I slept so well! It was so dark and quiet."

When I looked inquiring, she went on, "Joe always insists on our going to sleep with the TV and a light on. Even if he falls asleep and I turn the set off, he reaches right over and switches it back on."

She returned home, vowing to make some changes.

If you feel you have to have the television on in order to drift off, try going without it for a few nights, with the room completely dark. According to the National Sleep Foundation, "Flickering light and stimulating content can inhibit restful sleep." Any light disrupts the pineal gland's production of melatonin and serotonin. Computers in the bedroom don't add to a feeling of relaxation either, but for another reason. They are a reminder of work to be done and that there's an active, stressful world out there. Even exercise equipment can send messages you don't want to hear when you're trying to fall asleep.

Other Deterrents

There are other things that keep your bedroom from being the restful haven you need: piles of clothes; dirty laundry spilling out of a basket; chaotic dresser tops; untidy stacks of magazines, catalogs, newspapers, and other reading material; an unmade bed; ironing boards, hair dryers, and other appliances left out permanently; shoes you step on on your way to the bathroom; piles of "important" mail; glasses and coffee cups that have accumulated; closets so stuffed the doors can't be properly closed. If this is your bedroom, you probably avoid it except to collapse into bed at night.

WHAT DOES YOUR BED SAY ABOUT YOU?

If you've studied feng shui, you know that if you are in a relationship or want to be, you should have nightstands and lamps on both sides of the bed to signal equality and belonging, as well as sensual colors and not too many decorative pillows on the bed itself. I worked with a very attractive woman once who, despite a bitter divorce, told me she wanted a new relationship. Her Victorian-style bed was covered with so many small, lacy pillows and stuffed animals that it was obvious it was taken. Patsy lived near New York City and kept busy and happy meeting friends for dinner and the theater, caring for a college-age daughter who lived with her, and delighting in visits from her grandchildren. Despite what she said, bringing a man into her life did not seem a priority or even something she truly wanted.

The good news is that once you make your bedroom a haven, the room of your fantasies, it will be a lot easier to keep stuff from accumulating. In order to sustain the mood, you'll hang up your clothes when you take them off, bring in only what you want to read that night, and return dirty dishes to the kitchen in the morning. Once you have a space that you love and let that feeling take root, you'll do whatever you can to protect it.

Getting to Your Fantasy

Too many times the master bedroom becomes the dumping ground for all kinds of things, from baskets of clean laundry and piles of stuff to be mended and cleaned to bits of odd furniture. The rationale is that no one but you will see it and that the disorder doesn't matter so much because "you only sleep there." Surprisingly, people who keep the rest of their home looking perfect often let the bedroom go in this way. So your first job, before even considering your fantasy, is to get everything out of there or out of sight and put away.

Even if you use appliances, irons, or exercise equipment in the bedroom, cover them at night or put them away. Keep your makeup in a tray in your top dresser drawer or bathroom cabinet so that it can be completely out of sight. When you go to bed at night there should be no clothes or shoes visible except, perhaps, what you plan to wear the next day. Dresser tops need to have out only what belongs out.

Once everything is cleared away, you can get a clearer look at the room and see what you need to do to make it the bedroom of your fantasy.

Taking Action

Look around your bedroom. Decide what supports your mood and function and will stay. With items you decide will go but are still good, use the dot system. Put a blue dot on anything you want to offer to a specific person (write that person's name or initials on the dot), a green dot on items you want to give to charity, and a red dot on anything you plan to sell. Put a yellow dot on anything you plan to toss or recycle. If the yellow-dot items are small, you can get rid of them right away.

The Tyranny of Clothes

People often complain that they don't have enough closet space. The people who complain are just as apt to have walk-in closets and specialized systems as the people who don't. Even when there is room for everything, it is often all out of order and many nonclothing items have found their way in. And why not? With a huge closet, either your clothing expands to fit the space or you use the room to store everything else as well.

I have my own two rules for clothing: (1) have only as much as you can take care of easily and (2) have only as much as you can wear. That's it.

If you believe the closet system advertisements and the profiles of celebrity homes that show neat shelves of sweaters in every shade known to fashion, there are people who can care for and wear an endless amount of clothing. But I can't.

My old-fashioned closet is three feet wide and holds everything I wear, including shoes and jewelry in a hanging compartment bag. Besides a rod for hanging, I have four wire bins that slide out for sweaters and turtlenecks in the winter and T-shirts and shorts in the summer. My slacks and jeans are in three plastic boxes on the overhead shelf. I also have a rigid hanging holder on the side for dirty laundry. My jewelry is in a two-sided hanging bag that has thirty-two compartments on each side and allows me to find the piece I want immediately. But nothing is jammed into the closet or hard to find.

This is as much clothing as I can wear, hang up, put away, and keep clean. It wasn't always so, of course. In my twenties and thirties, not only did my mother give me complete wardrobes at Christmas and for my birthday, but when I visited her at other times, she always offered me some of her beautiful castoffs. My mother loved clothes but had no trouble keeping her wardrobe under control by giving things away promptly to people like me. The trouble was, the clothes I brought home were her style, not mine. But they were so lovely that I kept them in my closet and did wear some occasionally. Even though I needed a variety of clothes for work, the sheer volume of outfits jammed in my closets defeated me. Instead of getting hemmed or taken to the dry cleaner, clothes languished and died, unlamented.

Relief Spelled D-O-N-A-T-E

When I gave most of the clothing to charity, my giving was complicated by love and guilt. Yet I was drowning in a sea of fabric. On my first pass through, everything that I knew I would never wear, or wear again, went on the pile. The next time, it was things that needed some work before I could wear them, repairs I knew I wouldn't make. Eventually, I was left with the clothes I wore regularly and items that I actually liked. I ended up taking three large plastic leaf bags of good clothes to the Salvation Army store.

Not that I was done. I still had to think about what *my* style was. I was getting a good idea of what it wasn't, but that left a black hole. I consulted books, but I couldn't see myself as preppy, flamboyant, girl-next-door, or anything else exactly. It was a matter of trial and error and periodic trips to a wonderful thrift shop. By not paying much for the items I bought, I could donate them back if I decided they were mistakes.

Household Endangered Species #17
A set of highball glasses with a matching tray that you've never used because you don't serve cocktails. But they were a wedding gift.

Did I find a style? I hope so. I wear jeans and turtlenecks much of the time, a lot of black for dress with dramatic jewelry against a solid background, a few unexpectedly romantic outfits and vivid splashes of color. But I finally wear everything I own and feel good when I put it on.

Assessing Your Clothing Capability

I believe that the amount of clothing people can wear, care for, and keep under control varies widely. But life is easier when you find your level and know that everything in your closet fits and is ready to go and that you feel good wearing each item. For some reason, it's also easier to put clothing away after wearing it.

Looking in your closet you'll probably find things that were marked "Clearance," which you were tempted to buy because they were so cheap—how can you go wrong with a $4 sweater?—and you ended up with a lot of clothes you just don't wear. When I help people go through their closets, I'm no longer surprised to see how many items still have the price tags on.

TRIMMING THE TRIMMINGS

Sometimes when you can't decide whether a piece of clothing should stay or go, it helps to ask yourself some questions about it.

- **"Do I have a place to wear this?"** If you haven't been line dancing in fifteen years, are retired from your day job, or have no firm prospect to be invited to the Inaugural Ball, say good-bye to the clothing you are holding on to for those occasions. You'll feel much better moving into your current life. If you were invited to an important ceremony, you'd no doubt want something new to wear anyway.

• **"Would I buy this now?"** It may have made you feel chic or sexy or professional when you originally brought it home, but the glow is gone and the item feels outdated. It may be a clearance item that you never found the opportunity to wear. If it was a gift, ask yourself, "Would I buy this at all?" If not, then give it away.

• **"Do I feel attractive when I wear this?"** Sometimes you may reach for a particular outfit, thinking, "I haven't worn this in a while." But when you put it on and look in the mirror, you don't feel particularly uplifted. It looks OK but nothing special. Your next thought may be, "Well, I'm only going to work/ to that meeting/food shopping. It doesn't really matter." But it does. Whether you feel attractive affects your whole mood.

• **"Does it have sentimental value?"** Sometimes I encounter people whose closets are giant memorabilia boxes. They know they will never wear certain things again, but they have fond memories of the times that they did. They remember their earlier self as gutsy or daring or attractive. If it's decorative, I tell them to consider hanging it on the wall or putting it into a shadow box. If not, take a photo before you give it away.

Getting Started

Before choosing any clothing to recycle, you need to pick out three or four complete outfits that fit well and that you feel good wearing.

To do this you may even have to buy some accessories or additional items. But you need to know that you have a core wardrobe for any occasion. This will allay your fears that once you weed through your closet you will literally have nothing left. If you are confident that some clothes in the cotton jungle are better than the rest, you'll be able to make more objective judgments.

"I Paid Good Money for This!"

Heard that before? As discussed in Chapter 7, whether it's a Coach bag, a jacket that justified its price by promising "to go with everything," or that pair of shoes that hurt your feet, most closets have items sitting in them that are in the process of being depreciated. Additionally, they may also be promising that you'll use them "sometime." If your income fluctuates, they may be reminders of more flush times, and you may wonder if you'll be able to replace them.

But have faith that the good times will cycle back. By moving out items that are no longer an active part of your life, you are creating room for new and better things to enter. You are paring your wardrobe down to only as much as you can easily take care of and wear.

Putting It Together

Once you have dealt with your clothes and any external clutter, you are ready to re-create your bedroom. By now you probably have a good idea of mood and color. I've seen wonderfully restful bedrooms in blue and white, sensual settings in peach and yellow, bedrooms with luxurious bedspreads and drapes. Others have just the simple homeyness of patchwork quilts and bare wood floors. Whatever means rest, renewal, and pleasure to you is the right choice.

The larger your master bedroom or master suite is, the harder it will be to furnish. It can be difficult to create a sense of coziness and serenity if that's what you want, and nonbedroom items will clamor to come in and fill any empty space. If you already have a living room and den or great room, do you really need another living room where you sleep? It may be better to give the largest room to your children if they are still at home or turn it into an art studio—then use a smaller room to get the atmosphere and rest you need.

If you like to read before going to sleep or keep a glass of water, tissues, or other items handy, it's a good idea to have a bedside table with a lamp. Unless you have a walk-in closet with places for everything, each person sharing the bedroom needs a bureau or dresser. A comfortable chair is part of my fantasy, but if you are working full-time or raising an active family, you may not currently have the leisure to get much use from it. On the other hand, it represents a future promise.

Bedroom Mission Statement

Once you decide on the mood and functions and whatever you want to change, you will have a direction and can write your mission statement.

I want my bedroom to

_____

_____

_____

So I will

_____

_____

_____

Taking Action

Assess anything you need to do or buy, such as painting the walls or purchasing new linens, or anything else. Write them down here or in your notebook.

_____

_____

_____

18

Bathrooms:
The New Home Spa

An article in the *New York Times* Real Estate section in June 2006 discussed the phenomenon of home buyers spending several million dollars to buy houses in Brooklyn and then demolishing them to build mansions. While teardowns are not new, one story intrigued me. A 10,400-square-foot home was being built to include four bedrooms, five bathrooms, and three half baths, along with other amenities, such as a theater and exercise room. What could the purpose be in having twice as many bathrooms as bedrooms? Considering the fact that we spend less time in bathrooms than in any other room, why is it important to have so many?

When I asked that question, someone pointed out that bathrooms aren't that basic anymore. They have Jacuzzis, triple sinks, and Japanese toilets that weigh you, check your body mass ratio, and analyze the sugar in your urine. Everything short of a live-in masseuse, in fact.

Major Surgery

The ugliest bathroom I ever saw was in a house in Port Jefferson on Long Island. Mine, unfortunately. Built in 1952, the room was cramped, with baby blue fixtures, pink tiles all over the walls and ceiling, and brown trim. A thick Formica countertop stretched from the sink to over the top of the toilet. Despite repeated scrubbing, the frosted glass shower doors looked permanently grimy.

I don't know why we tolerated it for as long as we did. Perhaps it was because the fixtures worked and there seemed no way to change the colors short of gutting the room and starting over. Besides, we rationalized, it was only a bathroom. No one else saw it. The downstairs guest bathroom, which everyone else used, was more attractive.

But then a couple of the ugly bathroom's tiles came loose and the tub started to chip. It was time to make changes. We couldn't do anything about its size, but as soon as the sliding doors on the tub were removed, the room looked bigger. The Formica countertop went next, and a bathtub specialist replaced the sink, toilet, and bathtub with white fixtures.

The theme was old-fashioned, 1920s in white and deep blue, with a Tiffany "stained glass" window. I painted over the pink and brown tiles with waterproof white enamel and covered the floors with vinyl tile in an Art Deco design. For the focal point I enlarged a Tiffany window print, dividing it in sixteen pieces to fit over the small panes of glass, and then had sections of patterned Plexiglas cut to fit over those. The wood surrounding the glass was painted dark blue.

Household Endangered Species #18
One of a large group of facial masks and conditioners that haven't yet done what they were supposed to—but surely they will in the future.

If you decide you need to renovate, you don't have to spend a fortune unless you want to. You can do it for as little as the cost of attractive fixtures from a home improvement store and the price of their installation. You can even order a rigid cover that will slip over your old bathtub like a glove. Or you can go all out with a Jacuzzi, a heated floor, and ceramic or glass sinks. There are breathtaking designer basins on the market.

Getting in the Mood

Whatever you do, your bathroom should make you happy. Why not choose a theme that feels exciting? You can create a sensual retreat of candles and pastel hues like an expensive spa; a lush rain forest with varnished tree trunk slices and rocks surrounding the tub, huge plants, and leopard-printed towels; a beach house with a ledge for shells and starfish, striped deck chair, and watery-blue shower curtain; or a Victorian boudoir with tongue-and-groove wallboard, French prints, and lots of lace. Think Japanese, think Caribbean, think sophisticated, think nautical. Think whatever excites you!

The Big Purge

But before you get too creative, there are a few basics to follow. The first step is to discard all the outdated prescriptions, facial masks that didn't work, cute hotel-sized toiletries, shampoos you didn't finish, unloved aftershave, cosmetics that are wrong for you, and so on. In short, purge anything that you aren't actively using or know that you won't be using in the near future. Items that you use only once in a while—such as moleskin patches, Preparation H, poison ivy remedies, Dramamine, and so on—can be taken out of the medicine cabinet and stored in a drawer or basket, leaving adequate room for the everyday items.

If you feel you still don't have enough storage even with the free-loaders gone, consider a freestanding cabinet that fits in with your theme. There are also wire racks that fit above the toilet, mounted or standing, and shower caddies. If you use a caddy that hangs over the shower head, make sure the sides are high enough so that shampoos and other bottles do not come tumbling out.

Little Luxuries

Even if you aren't remodeling the bathroom or replacing outdated fixtures, you can still add some nice extras. Showerheads come with adjustable spray patterns. Handheld showerheads have built-in rollers that you can rub against your skin for a massage. If you live in a chilly climate or a humid one, an electric towel warmer will provide wonderful comfort when you emerge into cold air from your shower and will dry the towels as well. If you love baths, invest in a steel caddy that stretches across the tub and is sturdy enough to hold magazines, candles, and a cup or glass.

A Three-Step Program

With your bathroom or bathrooms, all it takes is a simple three-part plan to re-create the room.

1. Purge everything outdated or not currently in use, including ratty towels.
2. Clean everything thoroughly, from the bathtub grout to the corners of the medicine cabinet and behind the toilet.
3. Add anything that's needed, such as new towels, a shower curtain, storage towers or baskets, artwork, and spa materials.

If you have more than one bathroom, you can create a mission statement for each, if you want.

Bathroom Mission Statement

I want my bathroom to

_____

_____

_____

So I will

_____

_____

_____

Taking Action

There aren't a lot of bathroom items you will be giving away rather than discarding. But after you clear out and clean thoroughly, assess anything you need to change or buy and write them down here or in your notebook.

_____

_____

_____

_____

19

Rooms Great and Small

Dens and great rooms are the Mutt and Jeff of the home. *Den* implies small and sheltered, whereas *great room* sounds open-ended and expansive. Yet the main uses of each are for relaxing or spending time with family. You have endless freedom in furnishing these rooms, and they can handle more clutter than anywhere else in the house. The clutter should be temporary, of course, involving projects being done, materials being read or viewed, toys being played with, and should disappear each night or—at worst—at the end of each week.

Perhaps you'll want to do what my son, Andy, did. In his compact and child-centered house, the only free area was a finished basement room with a knotty-pine bar and a small refrigerator. Working with what was there, he gave this den a sports theme with autographed photos and baseball and golf memorabilia and then added a desk, a leather couch, a TV, and bookcases. It has the feeling of a masculine retreat, and although the twins are welcome down there, their toys are not!

Another family I know designed a great room with a tropical theme that was a nod to their West Indian roots. It has differentiated zones for eating, playing games, watching TV, and relaxing, but the whole is unified by leafy plants, rattan furniture, and light vibrant colors. An open raised counter divides the room from the kitchen. A common theme or colors keeps a great room harmonious even when you use it in many different ways.

But if you just let the den or great room evolve like a reality show, the strongest survivors will win out. And they may not be the ones you want. With no direction, an open-ended room can become a mishmash, a dumping ground for everything not having a designated place. The activities that belong there will spill over into the other rooms, and you'll be living in chaos.

In the example of the West Indian family, I mentioned the raised counter that divides the kitchen from the living area. This is an excellent idea. It mutes the sounds of food preparation; if the family eats in the great room, it shields the clutter of dirty pots and packages. With stools on the great room side, guests can sit and talk with the cook. Placing the eating area between the kitchen and the living part of the room is convenient and gives some psychological distance.

Above all, the room has to be comfortable. As James Lileks, author of *Interior Desecrations*, points out, "If you can't put your feet up on anything, it's not a den."

The only caution is to not make it a dumping ground for old couches, outdated furniture, and other items considered not good enough for the living room. A room that's a conglomeration of old stuff attracts other oddities and clutter faster than the speed of light. But you already knew that.

Easy Storage

Since the main purpose of this room is for pleasure, it makes sense to have what you are currently using readily accessible and to remove "guests" that have outstayed their welcome. If everyone has progressed beyond Candyland, there's no reason to store it any longer. Other household endangered species can include jigsaw puzzles that will never be finished, unidentified videotapes, orphaned craft materials, unloved books, last year's catalogs, and so on.

The emphasis in this room should be on easy storage—places to which things can be quickly returned and where they'll easily be found again. Shallow drawers and shelves are better than deep ones, and baskets and plastic bins that can be labeled are a good idea. If you have a clothes closet in the vicinity, fit it out with shelves or the stor-

Household Endangered Species #19
A collection of belts from when you were thinner that you plan on wearing again as soon as you lose a few pounds.

age towers with mesh metal pullouts such as IKEA sells.

Don't underestimate the importance of tables and flat surfaces to spread out projects, low enough if you have small children. Folding tables are a great idea for adults if you don't want them out all the time. The problem with using your dining table is that it doesn't allow for ongoing projects, such as jigsaw puzzles, gingerbread houses, or ship models.

Have Fun!

If you already have a living room and dining room or a dining area in the kitchen, you may decide to give your den or great room a specialized use. I've seen some that are media centers, complete with plush red chairs that recline, black walls, and framed movie posters. The audio and visual equipment is state-of-the-art. One family added a theater popcorn machine. The TV isn't left on constantly, and when the family settles down to watch a movie, it's an event.

In another den a pool table stands in the center of the room under several hanging, green-glass shaded lamps. The perimeter was given the look of an old billiards room, with comfortable leather chairs so that other people could sit comfortably and watch or read. Other great rooms have been pulled together with a country theme of hanging quilts, baskets, and old-fashioned school desks for the family's children.

Alternatively, I've seen totally up-to-date spaces with video games and flat-screen TVs and others with surfboard decor and lots of places to sprawl. If you have no interest in re-creating the past, go with a space age look and enjoy yourself.

"One-Eyed Monsters"

A word about television sets. If you have a den and keep the TV set in there, it doesn't impact other areas of the home where someone might want to read, do homework, or work on the computer. Having it in the great room is more problematic if it is on constantly. One solution is to house it in an armoire with the doors shut, turning it on only for specific programs. Another solution, if the room is large, is to erect clear, soundproof walls to mute the sound or even just screen off the area. If you feel you need a focal point, make it your fireplace or outdoor view instead of the TV.

GREAT ROOM POSSIBILITIES

It's important how you define your den or great room, so that it is actually used that way and does not deteriorate into a catchall. Here are some possible ways to use it:

- ■ Relaxing as a family
- ■ Eating informal meals
- ■ Working on crafts and hobbies
- ■ Gathering to read aloud

- Curling up with music and a book
- Watching TV and DVDs
- Playing with toys
- Napping
- Displaying art and your collections
- Using the computer
- Paying bills
- Storing media
- Playing games
- Accommodating overnight guests

After you consider the functions in the sidebar "Great Room Possibilities" and discuss it with other family members, write your mission statement.

Great Room/Den Mission Statement

I want my great room/den to

_____

_____

_____

So I will

_____

_____

_____

Taking Action

Look around the room, thinking about what is already in here that supports your mood and function and will stay. With items that will go but are still good, use the dot system (see Chapter 2).

Assess anything you need to do or buy, such as painting the walls or purchasing new furniture or accessories, and write them down here or in your notebook.

_____

_____

_____

20

"And This Is Our
Junk Room!"

I find the whole idea of junk rooms intriguing. They are rarely written into a blueprint with that designation, and they are never proudly introduced to company: "And this is where we put everything we don't know what to do with!" Rather, junk rooms become what they are by default, either because they were never given a name and use or because their past function became outdated and a new use was not created quickly enough. Even the old idea of a spare room sounds quaint, given the price of real estate, but an adult child's former room or a vaguely intended guest room can act like one.

The way to reclaim a spare room or junk room is, first, by naming it. When you refer to it as your art studio, sewing center, home office, meditation room, or darkroom, it becomes a place with that potential, one that just needs to be cleared out and refurnished. Sometimes it helps to actually put a sign with its designation on the door; doing that helps to keep anything else from being stored in there and will hold you to your purpose. The same principle can apply to a junk basement. Once it is given an identity, whatever is down there that doesn't fit must be removed or relocated.

A junk room can also be used for another very important purpose. When I talked about living rooms, I mentioned the importance of everyone living in the home having his or her own comfort area—at the least, a comfortable, well-lit chair. If there is adequate space, having your own room is even better. Children usually have their own rooms or, if they share a room, their own space in it. But when people are living together, one of them often stakes out a separate room

Household Endangered Species #20
Decorated coffee cups, most of which commemorate a vacation or holiday. Although most of them are never used, they need to be saved in case you ever have a large party and don't want to use Styrofoam.

for an office or the basement for a workshop, and the other doesn't realize it is important to do the same. But especially if you have compromised on decorating all the common rooms, you need somewhere to express what you want, a place to which you can retreat and which displays items that are important to you.

If a family member has no identifiable space, then the junk room is a perfect opportunity to create one.

WHAT'S IN YOUR JUNK ROOM?

After taking an informal survey, I find that these are the top ten occupants of junk or spare rooms:

1. Boxes that were never opened from the last move
2. Racks of out-of-season clothes, formal attire, skiwear, and so on

3. Christmas decorations, Easter baskets, and other holiday paraphernalia
4. The childhood belongings of adult children
5. Stacks of books, magazines, and photo albums
6. Spare suitcases and gym bags
7. Piles of fabric and other craft materials
8. Broken chairs, sewing machine cabinets, and miscellaneous tables
9. Older computers, window fans, vacuum cleaners, plastic laundry baskets
10. Empty cartons to use to send back defective appliances

Doing the Shuffle

Suppose you love ballet or ballroom dancing or something else that requires floor space and a mirrored wall. Perhaps you've always wanted to get together a group of friends and master the tango or Greek folk dances, but the largest open area was in your great room or basement. In that case, why not shuffle the rooms around and turn your junk room into a cozy den with your great room a dance hall? Or the oversized master bedroom could become your new dance floor and the spare room a more compact bedroom.

I've known several artists who abolished their dining rooms and made them into art studios because the light in the room was ideal. A concert pianist friend, Jeff, renovated a large storage area into a breathtaking space. It holds two grand pianos; he practices in his new studio and also gives lessons and informal recitals there. Another friend, Nancy, made sure when she moved into her new house that one of the rooms was furnished in a simple, peaceful way and used for meditation only.

Just because rooms have labels on a blueprint doesn't mean that they can't be called something else and used in a completely new way. Ben, the train collector I wrote about earlier, used his entire basement for his layouts. If you want a counseling or at-home consulting business or a room dedicated to selling on eBay or a large playroom for children or grandchildren, you may end up moving rooms all around. And why not?

If you feel yourself hesitating about unconventional use of your home, just ask yourself, "Whose house (or condo or apartment) is it anyway?"

To Guest or Not to Guest

There are pros and cons to using this space as a dedicated guest room. What I like about having one in the apartment is that it is always clean and ready and just needs a few minutes of perking up. It's probably an outgrowth of my own laziness. People can stay over on short notice, and there isn't the rush to put away everything from a room's other life. On the other hand, the room's very tidiness can make it a temptation to store items in it "just temporarily." We all know how that goes.

Another consideration is whether you are short on space. If you are, it doesn't make sense to use an entire room only once in a while, when you desperately need somewhere to make quilts or set up a home office or do aerobics. Inflatable double mattresses are quite sophisticated these days, and manufacturers have learned how to make convertible couches that are comfortable to both sit and sleep on. Don't sacrifice your own needs to create an image from *Gracious Living*.

First Steps

Before you can bring in anything to create the room you want, you need to move many things out. Remember that the items that ended up in your junk room or basement are either legitimate things that need storage somewhere or are hangers-on with one foot already out the door. This is a good time to use a decluttering technique called eyes of a stranger. Close the door to the room, take a short walk,

SETTING UP A GUEST ROOM

If you do decide that your junk room will be reborn to house company, here are some good things to fill it with:

- A comfortable bed or foldout couch with fresh sheets
- A flat surface to place toiletries
- Somewhere to hang or store clothes
- A place other than the floor for a suitcase
- A good light for reading and a second pillow for propping
- Fluffy towels
- A carafe and glass for water
- Fresh flowers
- Some snacks
- An alarm clock
- A choice of soft or firm pillow
- Some magazines and books
- A chaise longue or comfortable chair
- A good-sized mirror
- Pleasing art on the walls
- Blinds or curtains that make the room completely dark

You can take this as far as you like, to the point of terry slippers and robe, writing desk and chair, and the bed turned down with a mint on the pillow. But be prepared to institute a waiting list.

then come back and enter the room as if you were in someone else's house. You may start thinking things like the following:

- "Why are they keeping those old, rigid suitcases when they probably own lightweight ones with wheels?"
- "It would take a hundred years to use up all that fabric!"

- "Those computers are obsolete."
- "Why are they storing all this stuff for their kids?"
- "Who'd save a broken lava lamp?"
- "Does anyone really use _____ anymore?"

And so on. When you take an objective look at what is in there or down there, it gives you a valuable perspective and a direction to move toward.

Taking Action

Because some of the items you will come across will be bulky, this is a good place for using the dot system (see Chapter 2).

Chances are, your junk room has a function of sorts and even a mood, but they are not the ones you want. Think about what you would like the room to be instead and how you want it to feel. Then complete your mission statement.

New Room Mission Statement

I want this room to

_____

_____

_____

So I will

_____

_____

_____

Once the room is empty and you have an idea what you will need to make it into a crafts studio, home office, dance studio, guest room, or whatever you choose, write down here or in your notebook what you will need to do or buy to get to that point.

_____

_____

_____

_____

Step 3

Take Action

21

A Call to Arms

Every book on decluttering and organizing I've ever read advo-
cates the same method of sorting your belongings. That is, you
first gather together large plastic trash bags and sturdy cartons with
the following designations: trash; charity or tag sale; to be put away
later or returned to someone; items needing repair; and finally, an
indecision box for those things you aren't sure about letting go. Then
you go through your stuff and put everything in its proper category.

Sounds easy, doesn't it? Even people who have never heard of this
system could probably figure it out.

But if this universal method works so well, why is there still so
much clutter? I believe it's because this method approaches things
backward. Going in cold and stopping to decide what to do with
each item without any prior thought is exhausting and inefficient.
And who has unlimited time to do it?

By asking you to write down household endangered species and
other items at the end of each of the first eleven chapters, as well as
your rationale for saving them and, finally, a disposition, I wanted to
give you a jump start on the process. You were making the decision
then as to whether you should keep or dispose of your things, based
on seeing them in a new way.

When you were thinking about the way you wanted your rooms to be, you decided what furniture and accessories would support your goals, then you threw out or put identifying dots on anything that wouldn't. Thinking about items and what they mean to you helps to objectify them. Once that happens, you can make an informed decision.

Learning to See

Take the case of Frank, who has moved with his wife to a community where the landscaping is handled professionally. But what's in his garage? His old power lawnmower, electric hedge clipper, and leaf blower. Chances are, he is so used to having them in his life that he no longer even sees them.

But suppose he writes down "lawnmower and other tools" on an assessment sheet and answers "Why I'm keeping it" about each. Suddenly he's faced with bulky items he will never use again. His best justifications might be, "Because they aren't hurting anything" or "In case we buy a house in the future," something his wife swears will never happen, and which he doesn't want to do either. A more realistic answer would be, "No reason is good enough," allowing him to realize he has the option to let these obsolete pieces of machinery go and use the space for more current items.

Traci is only in her twenties but already feels overwhelmed by stuff. When she got engaged last year, one of the gifts she was given was a bagel slicer, an instrument that reminds her unpleasantly of a guillotine. When she assesses the reason why she's keeping it, she writes down, "Because my friend Anna

Household Endangered Species #21
Your favorite childhood game, missing a few of its pieces. But it can always be played by borrowing markers from other games.

gave it to me." Is it worth keeping something that she imagines will slice her finger off? She decides that, because she has already thanked Anna and appreciates the thought, she will simply discard this lethal accessory.

Paula, an acknowledged packrat, filled pages in a notebook when I worked with her. "You don't have a space for how I'll feel when I get rid of these things," she joked.

"Trust me," I told her. "It will be worth the pain."

Paula surprised me with her enthusiasm once she got started, listing and then giving up items and categories I wouldn't have imagined her parting with. When all the clutter in her kitchen junk drawers was gone, she stared at the bare wood she hadn't seen in years. "It's so beautiful," she whispered. "I don't want to put *anything* back."

Paula was a convert. "I'm obsessive now in the other direction," she told me recently. "I hardly bring anything home! But I don't ever want to go back to the way it was before. I never thought my life could feel so free!"

Naturally, I'm hoping that that's the response you will have.

Starting the Process

In the next chapter, I am going to lay out the dispersal options for you, with hints on making the process as easy as possible. Once you have had a chance to decide in which direction you want to go, you will look at your lists again and put the items where they belong. Think of it as a giant game. In order for this process not to stretch out indefinitely, I am also going to give you a timetable.

Finally, in Chapter 23, we'll look briefly at what's left and where to go from here. And then you will be ready to live in your wonderful new home!

22

Finding New Owners

In a recent workshop someone asked me, "Is it better to try and find a home for things or just toss them in the Dumpster?"

I told her honestly, "It's best to do whatever you can. If you can easily find places where stuff will be appreciated, you'll feel better about discarding the item(s). But if some things are in poor condition, or nobody wants them, just toss them. It's your life that's important, not the well-being of stuff that's past its prime!"

In my experience, you can obsess about finding a "home" for everything to the point that the job never gets finished. Caitlin, a young woman who loved bazaars and craft fairs, had shopping bags lining her bedroom walls, filled with things that would be perfect for friends, sisters, nieces, and grab bag gifts—when she got around to distributing them. But she was a busy department store buyer and never seemed to have time to organize or mail the items. Even the samples she planned to use as gifts never seemed quite right.

When I asked how long the things had been there, she giggled sheepishly. But we agreed that it was time for them to go. She decided that first she would go through, pick out enough items for each member of her extended family, and have a spontaneous grab bag at their next large gathering. Those things fit in two bags, which she stowed.

Everything else went to the assisted living community where her aunt was a resident to be used as bingo and raffle prizes.

Changing Times

Sometimes we forget that we're living in the twenty-first century, in the midst of a physical glut. If you don't believe we're about to be swamped, take a trip to one of the charity thrift stores. The furniture in them looks close to new, and, indeed, most charities will not accept anything showing wear. Take a walk down the gadgets and dishware aisle, and notice the decorative plates, coffee makers, mugs, and cute statues. The age of scarcity, when anything was appreciated, is long past. Look at the clothes—no scarcity there!

We've talked about the natural life cycle of objects. When something has been used up, or nearly so, its life is over and it can be discarded with no regrets. No one needs a stained cork or a cracked plastic anything, even though they may think they do. In such a situation you may tell yourself, "I'm glad someone can use it," but it isn't being used—it's just on life support for a little longer.

Giving to Family and Friends

It's natural to think of family members, friends, neighbors, or coworkers when you are scaling items down. Some of your discards will have heirloom value, and others are still useful. But screen items carefully before you offer them. While it's true you are not responsible for anyone else's hoarding, you already know the people in your life who will take *anything*. It really is kinder not to put temptation in their way.

If you are older and want to pass on a quantity of things with value or a nostalgia quotient, a very good resource is a book called *Who Gets Grandma's Yellow Pie Plate?* (available from the University of Minnesota for $12.50 plus shipping, 800-876-8636). This helpful workbook discusses a number of distribution plans and how to handle the various problems that arise. At the same time, don't forget good friends or neighbors who have admired particular things in your home and would be thrilled to have something of yours. They are often interested in items your children say they don't want.

An Alternate Giveaway

One of the most effective ways I've found to declutter quickly is to have a giveaway brunch. The first time we did this we invited a lot of friends over with the purpose of letting them take anything that we had put in the garage: china, decorative pillows, knickknacks, records and tapes, books, little-used appliances, sporting equipment, framed pictures, and "gifts" of all kinds. Although there was some preliminary peeking, everybody played by the rules. They waited until the doors were officially open and came away with at least one thing they really wanted.

Sometimes people advocate clothing swaps or other types of exchanges. But I'm wary of those in this situation, when your purpose is to declutter your home. You can come away with as much stuff as you had before. Better to just be the giver when you're trying to minimize things.

Selling Items

Fifteen years ago if you were selling items, your choices were to put an ad in the paper; contact an antique, book, or collectibles dealer; or have a yard sale and see items that were worth more sell for very little. Now there is eBay.

In the beginning the Internet auction was tricky to negotiate and uploading photos could be a chore. But over the years the site has become more and more user friendly, and now anyone with a digital camera or scanner can list items. The site will walk you through the process step-by-step, and there is software you can buy that will help you list multiple items more quickly. If you don't want to take the time to list and sell items yourself, there are eBay stores and eBay sellers who will do everything—from the pickup to the listing and shipping—for you. The percentage that they charge, usually anywhere from 10 percent to 30 percent, is worth it, in my opinion.

If you haven't seen an eBay seller or store advertised near you, you can go directly to the eBay website and find one in your area. Just click on "Site Map," which will take you to a page that has topics under "Selling Resources." Click on "Trading Assistant Program," and then click the link that offers, "Find a Trading Assistant near you."

Besides fetching a fair price, eBay is a good resource for assessing how much the things you own are currently selling for. Again, go to the website, and this time click on "Advanced Search," and check the box that says "Completed Listings Only." Type in a few descriptive words (keywords) about your item to conduct a search for similar items. You will be able to find out the actual prices at which comparable or identical things have sold. By looking at offerings currently for sale, you will be able to see what your competition is.

Traditional Methods

The traditional methods—such as advertising in your local paper, contacting a professional dealer, or having a yard sale—still work, of course. Again, there are professionals who will handle every aspect of a yard sale—including the pricing, preparation, and actual sale—for you (for a percentage). You'll find them in the Yellow Pages or in the newspaper classifieds under "Garage Sales." If what you have for sale is not worth their while, they'll give you hints for selling it yourself. There are books in your local library to help you, as well as online sites that can be found by typing in "have a garage sale" on Google.

If you simply want to get still-good items out of your life as quickly as possible, you can put them outside on the curb or in the alley. Most geographic areas also have websites like craigslist (craigslist.org), where you can describe and ask a modest price for your merchandise, or Freecycle (freecycle.org), where you can simply give things away to anyone needing a particular item. If you don't want people coming to your home, you can drop things off or arrange for pickup elsewhere.

Make a Donation

Donating your overflow to charitable organizations takes less time than selling it and gives your remuneration in the form of tax deductions. There are a multitude of organizations in your area interested in having particular things.

My friend Adele, a volunteer at the Central Park Zoo, told me one day that some of the workers brought in empty cardboard rolls because the monkeys like to play with them. I thought it was a wonderful way to use those tubes and wanted to mention it, then I realized that not everyone lives close to a zoo. But in fact, communities across the country have specialized organizations that can use supplies.

DONATING IN THE NEIGHBORHOOD

Every organization needs *something*, whether it be gardening equipment, *National Geographic* magazines, craft materials, canes and walkers, or something else. It's just a matter of finding out what. You could even ask your local newspaper to write and run a feature on unsuspected opportunities for donation. But you can start by asking some of the following people and organizations what they'd like to have.

- Elementary school teachers
- Sunday schools and churches
- Migrant organizations

- Music teachers
- Veterinarians
- 4-H clubs
- Aquariums
- Vocational shop teachers
- Elder day care programs
- High school art teachers
- Veterans' homes
- Volunteer ambulance companies
- Halfway houses
- Day camps
- Women's organizations
- Small theater groups
- Hospitals
- Big Sister/Big Brother programs
- Retirement communities
- Social services departments
- Girl Scout troops
- Rotary Clubs
- Preschool programs
- Thrift shops
- Dress for Success organizations

Who Wants What?

If you're still wondering what to do with specific items, here are some suggestions.

Books

We've already talked about what *not* to donate: older encyclopedias and dictionaries; outdated travel guides, computer how-tos, medical guides, and textbooks; shabby paperbacks; almanacs; and outdated cookbooks and instruction guides.

Thrift stores, senior centers, hospitals, prisons, and veterans' homes are happy to receive popular fiction and bestsellers, mass market paperbacks in good condition, romance novels, sports biographies, and humor and other light reading. Libraries prefer hardcover books, trade paperbacks, and nonfiction that is current and in good condition. If you have salable books of a specialized nature, consider organizations like Eco Encore (800-332-4483), which raises funds for environmental groups in the Northwest and can reimburse you for a certain amount of postage. Housing Works (212-334-3324) has a "book cafe"; proceeds are donated to charity.

Cell Phones

As of 2006, according to Collective Good, there were 750 million used mobile phones either sitting on shelves or in a landfill, even though the EPA has classified them as hazardous waste. Organizations such as Collectivegood.com refurbish cell phones and donate any profits to the charities you select. You can locate others by searching on the Internet.

Clothing

You probably already have some good resources for making clothing donations, such as Goodwill, Salvation Army, and local churches and synagogues. Rehabilitation and rescue missions need presentable clothing for residents who are interviewing for jobs as well as those already working. An increasing number of communities are collecting prom dresses for teenagers who cannot afford to buy them new.

If your clothing can be considered vintage, don't forget about high school and college drama departments and small theater groups, who often stage plays set early in the twentieth century. Items such as hats, gloves, suitcases, and anything that would make a good prop are welcome as well.

Computers

Several years ago it was difficult to find homes for used computers and accessories. But there are now several organizations dedicated to refurbishing still-working computers (and peripherals) and acting as a clearinghouse. Even if you have to pay for shipping, your donation is tax deductible. Two organizations that are currently active are the Used Computer Mall (usedcomputer.com) and Hearts & Minds (heartsandminds.org). You can also go to your search engine of choice and type in "donate used computer" to get a variety of resources.

Eyeglasses and Hearing Aids

Most people know that the Lions Club collects used prescription glasses and has collection boxes in libraries, community centers, Goodwill shops, and LensCrafters stores. But you may not know what happens to them after that. Once glasses have been collected, a machine reads the exact prescription and they are labeled and stored until they are a match for a resident somewhere in the world. More recently, the Lions have gotten involved in recycling hearing aids as well.

The largest recycler of hearing aids for people in need is an organization called Hear Now. Hearing aids should be packaged in a padded envelope and can be mailed to Hear Now, 6700 Washington Avenue South, Eden Prairie, MN 55344.

Fur Coats

If you are concerned about animal rights, you can send your old furs to PETA to use as teaching aids. The organization will accept furs for other purposes, such as bedding for orphaned baby animals that are being raised in wildlife shelters. Mail your furs to PETA, 501 Front Street, Norfolk, VA 23510.

Furniture, Appliances, and Household Goods
With so many furniture donations to choose from, thrift stores now have high standards for what they will accept. If your upholstered furniture looks like it's been around the block a few times but is still presentable, consider contacting homeless shelters or battered women's centers through your local social services agency. These groups are involved in helping people who are furnishing a home from scratch. Charities are happy to accept small working appliances and decorative items. By law they cannot take used mattresses.

Medical Equipment
Although prescription medications cannot be accepted, there is a need for wheelchairs, walkers, motorized scooters, hospital beds, crutches, and so on. Because of their bulk, which makes them difficult, and sometimes expensive, to mail, you are better off first trying to donate them to your local ambulance company, hospitals, clinics, or assisted living facilities. Sometimes the Multiple Sclerosis Society and the Rotary Clubs accept medical equipment as well. If you have no takers locally, two national groups that supply mobility aids around the world are Orphaned Wheelchairs (503-375-9523) and Wheels for the World (818-575-1743).

Musical Instruments
Your old flute has been languishing, unplayed, since . . . junior high? Some school districts can accept flutes, violins, trumpets, and other instruments directly, provided they are in good working condition. Other districts ask that you donate instruments through the music

store that supplies the schools' rentals. You can also try contacting private music teachers in your community to see if they have students who can't afford to buy their own.

Towels

Anyone who has taken a pet for treatment in a veterinarian's office knows how important towels are in handling the animals. They don't have to be in pristine condition either.

Toys

Children's toys, puzzles, books, and games not missing pieces, as well as ride-on equipment in good condition, can be donated to preschools and Head Start programs. Also consider homeless shelters, migrant camps, and charity thrift stores, as well as rummage sales sponsored by the PTA and other local groups.

Videos and DVDs

With the coming of DVDs, videotapes are taking a backseat at places such as veterans' homes, but they are still welcome at library and rummage sales. Most places that accept books will be happy to have videotapes and DVDs. Just make sure that videotapes and DVDs are original and not copies that you have made.

The Divine Dumpster

People laugh when I mention renting a Dumpster. They are afraid that it will be an admission to the world that they are out-of-control packrats. They also don't believe that they have enough stuff to fill one. Trust me, you do. In the unlikely event that you end up with any extra space, you can invite your neighbors to discard what they want in it. But I'm sure you'll be able to fill it by yourself. Stuff is bulky, and we all have more than we realize.

As far as what anyone else thinks of you, just tell them that you are remodeling—which is exactly what you're doing.

Renting a Dumpster is easy. One can be brought to you by your own garbage company if it is privately owned or from a company listed in the Yellow Pages under "Rubbish and Garbage Removal." The time for a Dumpster is as soon as you

Household Endangered Species #22
An electric fan that sounds creaky but still works. You don't use it much now that you have central air-conditioning.

have given family and friends any items they want, made your donations to charity, and/or had a garage sale. If your level of accumulation is like most Americans', you will have plenty of leftover items that are no longer perfectly good and, therefore, should be trashed.

An object is no longer perfectly good if no one wants it or if it requires work that won't be done. Rugs with stains or fraying edges, rusted outdoor furniture, heavy TV or stereo consoles, warped Ping-Pong tables and sports equipment, shabby upholstered furniture, broken baby furniture—and anything else you are unable to find a home for—are all fair game. Some computer equipment is just too old to be salvaged. Broken bikes won't be fixed by someone else. The odd-sized storm windows you saved after having combination storms and screens put on won't be reused. If no one will accept your heavy canvas tent, let it go without guilt, along with the cans of dried latex paint, the extra tiles from two jobs ago, the miscellaneous leftover pieces of wood, and that flimsy file cabinet.

One of the best things about a Dumpster is that it is right there and furnishes a place for the household endangered species you may have been on the fence about. Although no one wanted them, you thought you should do something with certain items. Now you have the opportunity. You can add the hand-me-down bureau you never liked, the lamp that keeps flickering on and off, the nonworking portable electric organ, outdated globes not old enough to be picturesque, and the furniture that has migrated to the basement, attic, garage, or shed. You'll find the emphasis has shifted from salvaging them to getting your money's worth from the Dumpster.

The Dumpster does not have to be a permanent addition to your lawn decor. You can have it delivered Friday, fill it up over the weekend, and have it removed on Monday. And then you will be free to take the final steps to creating the home you've always dreamed about.

CLEARING-OUT TIMETABLE

Although my plan is based on a three-step schedule, don't despair if it takes you longer than you expect to complete the process. Even if you get everything cleared out quickly, you may end up tweaking your rooms and making adjustments for some time to come. The timetable that follows is a suggestion that can keep you from getting mired in the process. It's helpful to write start and finish dates in your notebook or indicate on a calendar your deadline date for finishing each task.

- Trash should be gotten rid of as you go, except for large items, which will go in the Dumpster at the end.
- Books dropped off at libraries or thrift stores—one week.
- Items for charity—distributed to them within two weeks.
- Gifts to family and friends—two weeks, including shipping or pickup at your home.
- Garage sale or classified ad—three weeks.

- eBay items—picked up by seller within two weeks. If you want to sell smaller collectibles yourself over the next few months, isolate them in several cartons.
- The Dumpster should be filled within a week of being dropped off.

Like many prison sentences, these tasks can be done concurrently rather than consecutively. You've already made the decisions and marked the items with dots, so it should just be a matter of collecting them and sending them in the proper direction.

What happens if you try hard but can't reach a friend or find anyone who will take certain items? Accept the fact that you've tried, and either give the items to someone else or a charity or just trash them. If you don't act in a timely way, once the momentum has waned, you are in danger of living with your household endangered species forever.

23

Last Steps

You've identified the reasons for your complicated relationship with everything from dead batteries and your college calculus book to expensive shoes that hurt your feet and ragged cheerleader pompons. You've said good-bye to that bargain sweater, a thousand plastic bags, and the 1970s encyclopedia you inherited from your childhood home.

After doing all of that, you reimagined the rooms in your home in exciting ways. Next up is to do any repairs or painting, arrange the furniture and accessories that you've saved, and buy anything you need. Refer back to your mission statements or write them all on one sheet of paper for easy reference. Then finish your room transformations and photograph them.

My last suggestion is that you go through the notes you wrote down in this book or in your notebook and compile one final list. Toward the end of each of the first eleven chapters, you wrote down some reminders in case you were tempted to accumulate certain items in the future.

Take a loose sheet of paper and title it "Reminders." Then copy the goals you wrote, for example:

- "I can appreciate beautiful things without having to own them."
- "I will discard magazines as soon as the new issues arrive."
- "I won't let this bedroom become a dumping ground again!"

When you are finished, put this list in your top desk drawer, on a bulletin board, or someplace else where you will see it frequently. These attitude shifts are your strongest tool to keep your home beautiful and uncluttered in the future.

Revitalizing the rooms is as much fun as getting rid of hangers-on. But if you find yourself stuck with a decorating or decluttering dilemma or have other questions, feel free to write to me in care of McGraw-Hill. I'd love to hear about your household endangered species and see your before-and-after photos.

In a seminar last night, a young woman asked me, "Now that you've achieved the vacation house feeling, do you miss any of your stuff?"

My answer, "No," came so quickly that everybody laughed. But it's true. I'm so content with my environment, having the things I love around me, arranged in a way that lifts my spirit, that I don't ever think about what isn't here. I guarantee that you'll feel the same way!

Household Endangered Species #23
A group of old watches that have collected in your dresser drawer along with three cuff links, a broken ID bracelet, and some pennies. The watches don't work but are nice to look at.

Selected Resources

Just as libraries have expanded their offerings, there are many ways to get help, particularly over the Internet, which has decluttering sites and chatrooms too numerous to list. Here are a few valuable resources:

- The Container Store has stores all over America and also offers extensive products online at thecontainerstore.com. Call 888-CONTAIN for a store near you.
- FlyLady (flylady.net) will send you daily messages on how to keep your home clean and organized.
- Hold Everything is one of the original venues for organizing supplies. Phone 800-421-2285 for a catalog or the location of a store near you.
- Home Focus on Neat and Clean Living offers some unique storage and cleaning ideas. Call 800-221-6771 for a catalog of helpful products.
- HGTV, a cable television station, has a wide selection of programs on decluttering and decorating and stores them on their website, hgtv.com, for reference.

- Jeff Campbell's Clean Team explains how to have time left over for living by using intelligent methods and products. Call 800-717-2532 for a catalog or visit cleanteam.com.
- Lillian Vernon offers many organizing supplies as well as other interesting items. Visit lillianvernon.com or call 800-901-9291 for a catalog.
- National Association of Professional Organizers can be contacted at 512-206-0151. If you visit the group's website (napo.net), you can type in your zip code and see a list of professional organizers near you and the specific services they offer.
- Organize.com is a website that sells everything for organizing that you can imagine and a few things you never thought about.
- The Squalor Survivors (squalorsurvivors.com) website features dramatic before-and-after photographs and stories of people with too much stuff.
- Stacks and Stacks Homewares (stacksandstacks.com) has storage with a flair. Its retail store is located in San Francisco, but you can call 800-761-5222 for a catalog.

Selected References

Aslett, Don. *Clutter's Last Stand*. Cincinnati, OH: Writer's Digest, 1984.

Beckerman, Ilene. *Love, Loss, and What I Wore*. Chapel Hill, NC: Algonquin Books, 1995.

Collins, Terah Kathryn. *The Western Guide to Feng Shui*. Carlsbad, CA: Hay House, 1996.

Culbertson, Judi, and Marj Decker. *Scaling Down: Living Large in a Smaller Space*. Emmaus, PA: Rodale, 2005.

DeGraaf, John, David Wann, and Thomas H. Naylor. *Affluenza: The All-Consuming Epidemic*. San Francisco: Berrett-Koehler Publishers, 2001.

Dickson, Laurie E. *Artists' Interiors: Creative Spaces, Inspired Living*. Gloucester, MA: Rockport, 2003.

Ellis, Estelle, Caroline Seebohm, and Christopher Simon Sykes. *At Home with Books: How Booklovers Live with and Care for Their Libraries*. New York: Carol Southern Books, 1995.

Ferrer, Christy. *Breaking the Rules: Home Style for the Way We Live Today*. New York: Simon & Schuster, 2001.

Gallagher, Winifred. *House Thinking: A Room-by-Room Look at How We Live*. New York: HarperCollins, 2006.

Guthrie, Pat. *Interior Designer's Portable Handbook*. New York: McGraw-Hill, 2000.

Hammerslough, Jane. *Dematerializing: Taming the Power of Possessions*. Cambridge, MA: Perseus Publishing, 2001.

HGTV Books. *Design on a Dime*. Des Moines, IA: Meredith Books, 2003.

Jhung, Paula. *Cleaning and the Meaning of Life*. Dearfield Beach, FL: Health Communications, 2005.

Kasser, Tim. *The High Price of Materialism*. Cambridge, MA: The MIT Press, 2002.

Katillac, Kelee. *House of Belief: Creating Your Personal Style*. Salt Lake City: Gibbs-Smith, 2000.

Kingston, Karen. *Clear Your Clutter with Feng Shui*. New York: Broadway Books, 1999.

Llewelyn-Bowen, Laurence. *Fantasy Rooms*. London: Boxtree Macmillan, 1999.

Madden, Chris Casson. *A Room of Her Own: Women's Personal Spaces*. New York: Clarkson Potter, 1997.

Michels, Richard, editor. *Collector's Styles: Decorating with the Things You Love*. Des Moines, IA: Meredith Books, 2002.

Neziroglu, Fugen, Jerome Bubrick, and Jose A. Yaryura-Tobias. *Overcoming Compulsive Hoarding*. Oakland, CA: New Harbinger Publications, 2004.

Perle, Liz. *Money: A Memoir*. New York: Henry Holt, 2006.

Schor, Juliet B. *The Overspent American: Why We Want What We Don't Need*. New York: Basic Books, 1998.

Schwartz, Barry. *The Paradox of Choice: Why More Is Less*. New York: Harper Perennial, 2005.

Sher, Barbara. *It's Only Too Late If You Don't Start Now*. New York: Delacorte, 1998.

St. James, Elaine. *Simplify Your Life*. New York: Hyperion, 1994.

Susanka, Sarah. *Not So Big Solutions for Your Home*. Newtown, CT: Taunton Press, 2002.

Index